WALCH PUBLISHING

Daily Warm-Ups

U.S. HISTORY

Lisa French

Level II

The classroom teacher may reproduce materials in this book for classroom use only.
The reproduction of any part for an entire school or school system is strictly prohibited.
No part of this publication may be transmitted, stored, or recorded in any form
without written permission from the publisher.

1   2   3   4   5   6   7   8   9   10
ISBN 0-8251-4346-2
Copyright © 2002
J. Weston Walch, Publisher
P.O. Box 658 • Portland, Maine 04104-0658
walch.com
Printed in the United States of America

The *Daily Warm-Ups series* is a wonderful way to turn extra classroom minutes into valuable learning time. The 180 quick activities—one for each day of the school year—review, practice, and teach U.S. history facts. These daily activities may be used at the very beginning of class to get students into learning mode, near the end of class to make good educational use of that transitional time, in the middle of class to shift gears between lessons—or whenever else you have minutes that now go unused. In addition to providing students with fascinating historical information, they are a natural path to other classroom activities involving critical thinking.

Daily Warm-Ups are easy-to-use reproducibles—simply photocopy the day's activity and distribute it. Or make a transparency of the activity and project it on the board. You may want to use the activities for extra-credit points or as a check on the historical and critical-thinking skills that are built and acquired over time.

However you choose to use them, *Daily Warm-Ups* are a convenient and useful supplement to your regular lesson plans. Make every minute of your class time count!

Archaeologists use scientific processes to find out how old an artifact or a ruin might be. Two processes are frequently used to date archaeological findings. What are they? Use the clues below to identify two common dating methods.

_____

1. This method can only be used if the artifact is made of wood. _____

2. This method uses an element with a particular atomic weight. The element exists in all organic matter and breaks down at a constant rate.

_____

Where did the first North Americans come from?

Most historians believe that humans began coming to the North American continent from Asia during the Pleistocene era (the Ice Age). What else do we know about these early people?

Indicate whether each of the following is true or false. Be sure to read each statement carefully!

1. The first humans probably came to North America around 12,000 B.C.E. _____

2. These people may have crossed from Asia by a land or ice bridge over the Baltic Strait. _____

2

3. These first people were hunters who usually lived in stone huts. _____

4. They were meat eaters who dined on bison and other animals. _____

5. They hunted with flint-tipped spears and gathered nuts and wild seeds. _____

6. They used animal skins for warmth and for trading with other tribes. _____

The most advanced early civilizations in the Americas were the Maya, Aztec, Inca, Toltec, and Chibcha cultures. They did not have writing systems to formally record their history. Still, we know that they achieved many things between 500 B.C.E. and 500 C.E. Their achievements included basketry, agriculture, pottery, weaving, and copper smelting.

In which present-day country or countries did each of the following cultures live?

Maya _____

Aztec _____

Inca _____

Chibcha _____

Toltec _____

When Europeans first made contact with the native peoples of South America, they say many new things. They often adopted the South American words for these new things. Some of these words are part of the English language today. Read each numbered definition below. Try to guess which English word of South American origin it refers to.

4

1. A tropical tree of the sumac family with edible, kidney-shaped nuts

_ _ _ _ _ _

2. A tropical cyclone with very high winds, often with heavy rain

_ _ _ _ _ _ _ _ _

3. A fireplace or pit over which meat and fish are cooked; also, the meat that is cooked over such a fire

_ _ _ _ _ _ _ _

4. A hanging couch or bed, usually made of netting, that swings from cords attached at each end

_ _ _ _ _ _ _ _

Although they were continents apart, the pre-Columbian natives of Mesoamerica and South America had much in common with their contemporaries in Asia. For example, the Maya had tools, cultural pastimes, and weaponry similar to those of some Asian peoples.

Which of the following did the Maya share with Asian cultures? Check all of the items below that were part of Mayan culture.

_____ bow and arrow

_____ wheel

_____ pottery

_____ game like Hindu *parchesi*

_____ steel implements

_____ boats made from reeds

_____ built-up wooden boats

5

The following statements about the Maya civilization are out of order. Number them 1 to 7 in the correct chronological order, with 1 being the earliest event.

_____ (a) Maya civilization reaches its height in about 1100 C.E.

_____ (b) The Maya empire is located in Guatemala, in cities built of stone.

_____ (c) The Toltecs absorb Maya culture.

_____ (d) Aztecs invade from the north, reaching Mexico City around 1325.

_____ (e) Toltecs invade from the north, led by King Quetzalcoátl.

_____ (f) Moctezuma II is conquered by Hernando Cortés.

_____ (g) The Maya empire moves to the Yucatán.

6

Native Americans were generally very welcoming to the first Europeans they saw in the fifteenth and sixteenth centuries. They introduced the newcomers to many agricultural products.

Place a check mark next to all the products that Native Americans gave Europeans.

_____ maize

_____ tobacco

_____ chocolate

_____ bananas

_____ horses

_____ coffee

_____ rice

_____ peanuts

_____ cassava

_____ wheat

_____ oats

_____ kidney and lima beans

7

A number of English words come from Mesoamerica. One source was Nahuatl. This language was spoken by many of the native peoples with whom the Europeans first made contact. Try to guess which Nahuatl-based words are being defined below.

1. A food or beverage made from ground, roasted cacao beans _ _ _ _ _ _ _ _ _

2. A plant of the nightshade family, grown for its red-orange, nonsweet fruit _ _ _ _ _ _

3. A small wolf native to North America _ _ _ _ _

4. A hot pepper, often used as a salsa ingredient _ _ _ _ _

8

Sixteenth-century Europeans were impressed when they first saw the pre-Columbian stone temples of Guatemala, the Yucatán, and Peru. However, they assumed that these structures must be Phoenician or Egyptian in origin. Why? Give at least two reasons for this assumption. Consider the physical appearance of the structures and European attitudes toward the peoples of the Americas. Explain your answer in one clear paragraph.

9

Some of the early peoples who lived in the valleys of the Ohio River and upper Mississippi River were known as the Mound Builders. The tribes sharing this culture are believed to have existed for hundreds, perhaps thousands, of years. Some artifacts that remain from these early peoples include carved stone pipes, simple hoes made of stone or shell, and ornaments of shell, bone, and copper. The Mound Builders were accomplished metalworkers. Historians call them Mound Builders because of the huge earthen mounds they left behind.

What were these mounds used for? What did they look like? Explain your answer in one clear paragraph.

10

At the time of European contact, some of the most highly developed tribes in North America were those of the northwest coast. They inhabited areas from present-day Alaska south to Oregon. These tribes wove baskets that were tight enough to hold water—even for boiling foods. They also carved totem poles. These were like decorative "family trees" that told who the owners were and from whom their family was descended. This trading culture allowed individuals to accumulate wealth and to inherit property.

What natural resource played the most important part in this Native American economy? What way of treating this resource was developed that improved the culture's well-being? Write two or three sentences to explain your answer.

11

The Pueblo peoples of North America developed a sophisticated culture. It survived for hundreds of years—from at least 217 B.C.E., with the early Anasazi tribes, to the Spanish invasion of 1540. Their adobe-walled towns can still be seen today in New Mexico and Arizona.

Three of the most important periods in the Anasazi culture are listed below. Number them 1 to 3 in the correct chronological order, from earliest to most recent.

_____ (a) The Basket Makers make pottery, but without the potter's wheel. They weave fabrics from plant fibers and make jewelry using seeds, shells, and turquoise. They develop the bow and arrow for hunting and defense.

_____ (b) In the Golden Age of the Anasazi, they build terraced cliff house communities with communal halls. They create black-on-white pottery and more elaborate woven baskets.

_____ (c) The Basket Makers live in caves or adobe huts. They weave baskets for storing wild seeds and little ears of maize. They also keep dogs and hunt with flint-headed spears. They generally wear no clothes except for sandals and fur in cold weather. Many remains of their dead survive, since they were buried in dry caves.

12

Many Algonquian words have found their way into English. Try to guess what the following Algonquian words are, based on the definitions below.

1. A large, antlered North American deer, related to the reindeer; also a town in northern Maine _ _ _ _ _ _

2. Hulled corn with the germ removed, often used in hot cereal in early North America _ _ _ _ _ _

3. A North American hardwood tree related to the walnut; its tough wood gave rise to one of Andrew Jackson's nicknames _ _ _ _ _ _ _

4. A small, striped American squirrel _ _ _ _ _ _ _ _

13

According to legend, the Mohawk chief Hiawatha formed the Iroquois League of the Five Nations in about 1570. This sort of alliance between Indian tribes was unusual. Most Native American groups were independent and somewhat isolated from each other. However, the Iroquois League was especially important in the seventeenth century, as European settlement threatened the natives' land and ways of life. In fact, the Iroquois were known as the fiercest fighters in North America.

Name the five tribes in this league.

14

A sixth tribe joined the league in 1712. Which tribe was it?

The opening words of a colonial-era Iroquois treaty with another tribe were translated this way: "We the people, to form a union, to establish peace, equity and order . . . ."

John Routledge, who attended the Constitutional Convention in 1787, was an admirer of the Iroquois people. He introduced these words to the assembly because he found them so impressive.

Do these words sound familiar? What similarities do you find between them and another important document? Write one or two sentences for your answer.

Do you think there is anything wrong with "borrowed" ideas or language as long as it is not copied word for word? Write a clear paragraph for your answer. Support your opinion with convincing reasons.

15

Before Europeans arrived, many different peoples lived in North America. Their clothing, housing, food, and cultures varied, depending on where they lived. Name at least four American Indian groups who once lived in each region below.

A. Northeast

_____

_____

_____

_____

B. Southeast

_____

_____

_____

_____

16

C. Northwest

_____

_____

_____

_____

D. Southwest

_____

_____

_____

_____

E. Plains and Central

_____

_____

_____

_____

Choose one Native American tribe to briefly research, either independently or with a group. Spend 10 or 15 minutes gathering your information using the Internet or other classroom resources. Then summarize your findings orally to the class.

17

Vasco da Gama of Portugal chose to sail south and east in 1497. Ferdinand Magellan of Spain chose to sail west in 1521.

Compare and contrast the results of da Gama's and Magellan's trips. What did each navigator find? What did each gain for his country? Write your answer in a clear paragraph.

18

These important maritime events are listed out of order. Write the date of each event on the appropriate line beside the event.

____ (a) Amerigo Vespucci claims to discover continental America, which is later named after him. He never actually commands any of the voyages he describes.

____ (b) Cristoforo Colombo (Christopher Columbus) explores the Virgin Islands.

____ (c) Giovanni Caboto (John Cabot) reaches the coast of what he hopes is northern Asia. It is actually northeastern North America (probably Newfoundland).

____ (d) Columbus explores the coast of Central America during his last voyage.

____ (e) Norsemen in Viking warships land in "Vinland," probably maritime Canada.

____ (f) Columbus lands at San Salvador.

____ (g) Juan Ponce de León reaches Florida on his search for the fountain of youth.

19

England did not play a significant role in the exploration of North America during the fifteenth and sixteenth centuries. In one sentence, explain England's lack of involvement during the early years of exploration.

_____

20

The caravel was invented by the Portuguese in the fifteenth century. It was instrumental in the Europeans' arrival in the New World.

What is a caravel? What innovations did it represent? How specifically did it help Europeans' exploration? Write one clear paragraph for your answer.

21

When Cristoforo Colombo—or Christopher Columbus—set sail from Spain on August 3, 1492, he brought with him a scholar who spoke Arabic.

Why did Columbus think this was necessary? Explain your answer as fully as possible in two or three sentences.

22

When Columbus first arrived in the Caribbean region in 1492, the population on the island of Hispaniola was about 300,000. Fifty years later, this population was virtually gone. So was most of the population of the Bahamas.

What were the causes of this population change? What unfortunate practice did this population drop lead to in the New World? Explain your answer in one clear paragraph. Be as specific as possible.

23

Giovanni Caboto (known to English speakers as John Cabot) was an Italian sailor. He was given permission by King Henry VII of England to sail on a voyage of discovery. Cabot intended to claim any otherwise unclaimed lands for England. In return he would make a nice profit on any trade he could arrange. In June 1497, this navigator and his three sons landed on the northeast coast of North America. Unfortunately, Cabot (and the king) considered his trip a near failure. Instead of the Orient, with its gold and spices, Cabot found only a rocky, heavily wooded coast. However, Cabot did notice one plentiful natural resource that both the Portuguese and the French were eager to begin trading as soon as possible.

24

What was that resource? Why did some Europeans consider it so important? Write one or two sentences to explain your answer.

Hernando de Soto was the first European to cross the Mississippi River. In 1542, he and his men were camped by the Mississippi. All around them were resentful American Indians. De Soto, who was ill, suddenly died. Here is the story of what happened to his body, according to a Renaissance Spanish historian:

. . . [The Spanish] determined to conceal what had happened from the Indians, for de Soto had given them to understand that the Christians were immortal; . . . although they were at peace, should they know him to be dead, they . . . might venture on making an attack. . . . [The officer] directed the body to be put secretly into a house . . . thence it was taken at night . . . to a gate of the town, and buried within. The Indians, who had seen [de Soto] ill, . . . suspected the reason; . . . they observed the ground loose, and . . . talked among themselves. This coming to the knowledge of [the Spanish officer], he ordered the corpse to be [dug] up at night, and . . . it was taken out in a canoe and committed to the middle of the stream. . . .

What happened to de Soto's body? Why did his soldiers do this? Write one or two sentences to explain your answer.

25

The Spanish were the first Europeans to explore North America. However, Spain did not develop strong colonies in North America, as England did.

Why did Spain not set up strong, self-sufficient colonies? Consider motive, local economy, and other factors in your answer.

26

In 1587, 117 colonists arrived in North America. They settled on Roanoke Island (in present-day North Carolina). This was the second English attempt to colonize Roanoke. By 1590, Roanoke Island was once more abandoned. All traces of the English settlers had vanished—except for the mysterious word CROATOAN, carved into a tree trunk. There are many theories about what happened to these early colonists. Still, no one is really sure.

Why was the Roanoke colony almost doomed to fail, while other colonies did so well? Consider climate, the native population, and support from England. Write one clear paragraph for your answer.

27

By the beginning of the seventeenth century, France controlled a vast region of North America. It stretched across southern Canada and down the entire Mississippi River valley to New Orleans. However, by the middle of the eighteenth century, French control of North America had greatly diminished (and would soon end).

Why was this the case? Write a clear paragraph to explain your answer. Be as specific as possible.

28

When England turned its attention to the New World in the seventeenth century, it set up many colonies. Beside each colony, write the name of its founder. The names of the founders are in the box below.

Lord Baltimore	John Smith
William Bradford	Roger Williams
John Hooker	John Winthrop

1. Jamestown (1607) _____

2. Plymouth (1620) _____

3. Massachusetts Bay (1630) _____

4. Maryland (1633) _____

5. Hartford (1636) _____

6. Providence (1636) _____

29

All the European countries had many reasons for establishing settlements or financing explorations in the New World. England was no different.

Name at least three reasons for England's commitment to colonization in the seventeenth century. Consider conditions in England at the time, religion, and economic factors in your answer. Explain your answer in a clear paragraph.

30

The Jamestown colony was started in 1607 by 120 men and boys. Within the first year, more than half of them died. The arrival of new supply ships, and the friendship of Native Americans like Powhatan, helped the colony survive. Since there were few women in Virginia at the time, however, the colony grew very slowly.

In 1619, an English ship arrived at Jamestown with 90 young, unmarried women. They were available as wives to settlers who could pay the shipping company 150 pounds of tobacco for the cost of the voyage.

What do you think happened when the women arrived? Write your predictions in one clear paragraph. Be sure to explain your reasons for what you think happened.

31

In 1619, a Dutch ship arrived in Virginia with a new trading commodity. Twenty of these were sold to Virginia settlers. With the arrival of this Dutch ship, the New World began a new chapter in its history.

What did the Virginia settlers buy? Write your idea below. Then compare answers with your classmates. Did some of you have the same answer?

32

The Pilgrims were originally in serious debt to their sponsors in England. These sponsors had financed the *Mayflower's* journey and the first settlement at Plymouth. The Pilgrims were eventually able to pay off their debt and gain ownership of the colony's land. They were even able to set up three new branch trading posts—one on the Kennebec River, one at the site of the present-day Cape Cod canal, and one at Hartford, Connecticut.

How did the Pilgrims earn enough money to pay off their debt? Why did they choose to set up new trading posts where they did? Explain your answer in two or three sentences.

33

Many of the early colonists were British.
However, people from other parts of Europe were also daring enough to try life in the New World.

For each colony listed below, write the name of the country (or countries) or colony its original settlers came from. Also write one or two sentences explaining why the colonies were first established.

1. New Hampshire (1638)

2. Delaware (1638)

3. North Carolina (1653)

4. South Carolina (1663)

5. New Jersey (1664)

6. Pennsylvania (1682)

7. Georgia (1732)

34

There were some distinct differences between French and British relations with the Indians in North America. These differences were based (at least in part) on each country's motive for being in the New World, as well as on lifestyle and location.

List at least three differences between the relationships the French and the British had with American Indians. Then write a clear paragraph explaining which approach you think worked better. Support your opinion with examples.

35

The women named in the box below were well known at some point in colonial America. Match each name with the appropriate description below.

(a) Henrietta Johnson	(c) Pocahontas
(b) Rebecca Nurse	(d) Elizabeth Timothy

1. She was the first American woman to publish a newspaper—the *South Carolina Gazette*—which she took over after her husband's death in 1738. _____

2. Convicted of witchcraft in 1692 in Salem Village, Massachusetts, this villager was one of 19 to die during the Salem witch trials. _____

3. The daughter of Native American chief Powhatan, she saved the life of John Smith in Jamestown in 1614. She later married British colonist John Rolfe and became Lady Rebecca. _____

4. She was the first woman painter in the American colonies, making her professional debut in South Carolina in 1707. _____

The major groups of colonies in North America are listed in the box below. The differences between these groups had to do with climate, natural resources, religious views, economy, and other factors.

| New England colonies | Middle colonies | Southern colonies |

Match each numbered description with the appropriate region.

1. Most people here belonged to the Church of England. Religion did not play a big part in daily life. Natural resources included rich farmland, fish, and lumber. There was some manufacturing: rum, lumber products, and naval products. These colonies exported grain to Europe and imported most foreign items they needed from Britain. _____

2. People here had a variety of religions. Natural resources included rich farmland, fish, fur, coal, iron ore, and lumber. Iron products were made here, and iron was exported to England. Grain and livestock were exported to other colonies. Imported goods came from Europe. _____

3. Religion controlled society here. Fish, fur, and lumber were the best natural resources. Ships and ship products were built here. Molasses and grain were imported from the Caribbean and other colonies; rum was made from the molasses and then exported. _____

37

Climate plays a vital role in shaping the history, culture, economy, and even the character of a particular place.

Read the three regional climate descriptions. Then decide which region is being described below.

(A) New England: cold, with long, harsh winters and short, mild summers; rocky soil, rather poor for most crops	(B) The middle colonies: cold winters, but not as harsh as New England's; summers longer and hotter than New England's; rich soil	(C) The Southern colonies: warmest climate—long, hot summers and short, mild winters; rich soil

38

_____ 1. These were known as the Breadbasket Colonies because they produced so much grain.

_____ 2. Towns were slow to develop; most people lived on large farms.

_____ 3. This region's growing season was shorter than South Carolina's, but longer than Connecticut's.

_____ 4. People turned from farming to the sea to earn their living.

_____ 5. Pneumonia was a risk factor for people who didn't have good shelter.

_____ 6. Farming was very profitable, so this area never fully developed its other natural resources.

_____ 7. Both farming and fur trading were very profitable in this region.

_____ 8. This area had the shortest growing season.

Two out of three of the major colonial groups in early America were involved in **triangular trade** with other countries. Which two groups were they? Check them below.

New England colonies _____

Middle colonies _____

Southern colonies _____

Compare and contrast these two triangular trading systems. Which continents and countries were involved? What commodities were traded? How did these commodities move from one place to another? During what period of time did each triangular trading system occur? Write one clear paragraph about each system that answers these questions.

39

© 2002 J. Weston Walch, Publisher

For each definition below, choose the appropriate word or phrase from the box. Not all words in the box will be used.

agriculture	discount	manufacturing
apprentice	exports	mercantilism
colony	imports	republic

1. Trade goods that are purchased from another country or colony

   _____

2. Someone learning a skill or trade from a master craftsman

   _____

3. A place that is settled by people from another country and is governed by the original country

   _____

4. Making products to sell to others

   _____

For each definition below, choose the appropriate word or phrase from the box. Not all words in the box will be used.

exports	indentured servant	tariff
governor	mass production	tea tax
imports	mercantilsm	textiles

1. Trade goods that are sold to other countries or colonies _____

2. A tax placed by government on imports or exports _____

3. Woven cloth or fabric _____

4. Someone who is bound by contract to work for someone else for a certain period _____

41

Boston had a newspaper as early as 1690. Virginia, however, had no newspaper until the *Virginia Gazette* was published in 1736.

Why did Boston start publishing newspapers so much sooner than Virginia? Write a paragraph that compares the two colonies in this respect. Include such factors as type of economy, population distribution, and education in your answer.

42

The British Parliament passed the Navigation Acts in 1660. These acts were designed to raise money for England. In some cases, they helped the colonies as well.

Look at the statements about the Navigation Acts below. Decide whether each statement represents a benefit for Britain, the colonies, or both. Circle the letter of your choice.

1. Only ships built in England or its colonies could carry goods to and from the colonies.
   (a) Helped Britain   (b) Helped colonies   (c) Helped both

2. All goods being sold to the colonies from other countries, or from the colonies to other countries, had to pass through Britain first for inspection and tariffs.
   (a) Helped Britain   (b) Helped colonies   (c) Helped both

3. Britain could only buy tobacco from its colonies.
   (a) Helped Britain   (b) Helped colonies   (c) Helped both

4. Britain could only import resources and manufactured goods that were not already available in Britain.
   (a) Helped Britain   (b) Helped colonies   (c) Helped both

43

Match each sport with its description below.

bowling	foxhunting	horseshoes
fencing	horse racing	lacrosse

1. This nonaerobic activity was played on the lawns of Jamestown, Virginia, starting around 1611. _____

2. This animal sport was formally organized in North America in 1665. _____

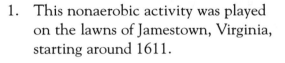

3. Adult Native Americans played this ball game as early as 700 C.E. _____

4. A school for this gentleman's sport was established in Boston in 1673. _____

5. This aristocratic activity was practiced mostly in the middle and southern colonies. _____

6. Both boys and girls could play this tossing game in mid-seventeenth-century America. _____

Most of the sports played today in the United States were originally "borrowed" from other countries. Match each sport (followed by the date it was introduced to America) with its country of origin.

1. Bermuda   (a) polo (1876)

2. England   (b) ice hockey (1893)

3. Germany   (c) handball (1882)

4. Ireland   (d) badminton (1890)

5. Canada   (e) lawn tennis (1874)

6. England   (f) skiing (1872)

7. Austria   (g) gymnastics (1825)

45

The enormous Central Plains area of the United States (the Mississippi River basin) was easily navigable in the nineteenth century. This was because of a network of rivers that flow in a more or less east-west direction. This was the direction in which most pioneers and settlers were headed. Thus, these rivers facilitated the settlement of the Midwest and, later, the West.

Write the names of the eight rivers of the Central Plains. Then check your list against a classroom atlas or other resource to see how accurate you were.

46

Many North American rivers (like those flowing through the Central Plains) have a general east-west direction. However, some major rivers in the United States flow basically north-south.

Name the three rivers with a north-south flow that influenced early American exploration and settlement.

47

Gottlieb Mittelberger came to America in 1750. Here is part of his description of crossing the Atlantic Ocean.

That most of the people [on the ship] get sick is not surprising, because . . . warm food is served only three times a week. . . . Such meals can hardly be eaten, on account of being so unclean. The water which is served . . . is often very black, thick and full of worms, so that one cannot drink it without loathing, even with the greatest thirst. Toward the end we were compelled to eat the ship's biscuit which had been spoiled long ago; though in a whole biscuit there was scarcely a piece the size of a dollar that had not been full of red worms and spiders' nests.

Imagine being a passenger on this ship. What drives you to make this journey? How can you survive the trip? Write a paragraph about your situation.

48

The Treaty of Paris was signed in 1763. This formally ended the French and Indian War. Among other things, it gave all France's former holdings in Canada to Britain. Here is part of the treaty:

[The King of France] renounces all pretensions . . . to Nova Scotia or Acadia . . . and guaranties the whole of it . . . to the King of Great Britain; Moreover, his Most Christian Majesty cedes . . . to . . . [the King of England] . . . Canada, with all its dependencies, as well as the island of Cape Breton, and all the other islands and coasts in the gulph and river of St. Lawrence. . . . [T]he French inhabitants . . . may retire . . . wherever they shall think proper, and may sell their estates, provided it be to the subjects of his Britannick Majesty. . . . The term limited for this emigration shall be fixed to the space of eighteen months. . . .

Where was Acadia? What happened to the Acadians who were forced to leave Canada within 18 months? Write a clear paragraph for your answer.

49

The French and Indian War was a struggle

between France and England for dominance in North America. Both wanted more land for colonization and trade.

Match each date with the event.

| 1754 | 1755 | 1756 | 1758 | 1759 | 1763 |

(a) The Treaty of Paris cedes all French power in North America to the British. _____

(b) The British attack Quebec City and win the battle, but British general Wolfe dies, as does French general Montcalm. _____

(c) The British lose this major battle; General Braddock is killed, but Colonel George Washington takes command. _____

(d) The French outnumber—and defeat—a force led by Lieutenant Colonel George Washington. _____

(e) In their first major victory, the British take control of Fort Duquesne, the hub of French activity in the Ohio Valley. _____

(f) The British lose this huge attack on Fort Carillon, situated between Lake George and Lake Champlain, although they will gain this fortress the following year. _____

50

Daily Warm-Ups: U.S. History

In the French and Indian War, the British allied themselves with the colonists. The French joined forces with the Indians. The war involved battles ranging from Quebec to Pennsylvania and lasted for nine years. The Treaty of Paris officially ended this long North American war.

How did the Treaty of Paris affect later history? In what condition— and frame of mind—did this agreement leave both the winners and the losers? Write one clear paragraph for your answer.

51

Who were some of the early participants in the American Revolution? Match each event of 1775 on the left with the key player in that event on the right.

1. On April 19, this captain led about 70 Minutemen on the Lexington village green in the first battle against the British. _____

2. Along with Paul Revere, he was asked by Boston's Committee of Safety to ride through the countryside warning people that the British were coming. _____

3. This major led 700 British soldiers from Boston Common to Lexington and Concord on April 18. _____

4. One of three "midnight riders" who were stopped by the British, he was the only one to slip through to warn the people of Concord that the British were coming. _____

(a) William Dawes

(b) John Parker

(c) Samuel Prescott

(d) John Pitcairn

How well do you know the early participants of the American Revolution? Match each event of 1775 described on the left with the key player in that event on the right.

1. With his Green Mountain Boys, he helped capture Fort Ticonderoga in New York from the British on May 10. _____

2. He was commissioned a general and commander-in-chief of the Continental Army on June 17—the day of the Battle of Bunker Hill. _____

3. Originally from Connecticut, this man led Massachusetts volunteers to help capture Fort Ticonderoga. He later joined the British side, betraying the colonists. _____

4. This governor received orders from England on April 14, 1775, to suppress the "open rebellion" in the Boston area, even if it meant using force. _____

(a) George Washington

(b) Benedict Arnold

(c) Thomas Gage

(d) Ethan Allen

53

Match each famous Revolutionary-era quotation in the left-hand column below with the person who said it on the right.

1. "There, King George will be able to read that without his spectacles." _____

2. "We must all hang together, or assuredly we shall all hang separately." _____

3. "I know not what course others may take, but as for me, give me liberty or give me death!" _____

4. "We have no other alternative than independence, or the most ignominious and appalling servitude." _____

(a) Patrick Henry

(b) Benjamin Franklin

(c) Sam Adams

(d) John Hancock

54

"[It is foolish] . . . to be always running three or four thousand miles with a tale or petition, waiting four or five months for an answer, which when obtained requires five or six more to explain it in."

Thomas Paine made this statement in 1776. To what was he referring? How did the communication and transportation systems of that era affect the situation that Paine is describing? Write a clear paragraph for your answer.

55

© 2002 J. Weston Walch, Publisher

For each definition below, write the appropriate word from the box. You will not use all the words in the box.

allies	militia	smuggling	treason
boycott	repeal	Tories	Whigs

1. The crime of working to overthrow the government _____

2. Refusing to buy a particular product or service in order to force changes in a business or law _____

3. Groups or nations that agree to help each other _____

4. To cancel a law _____

56

Test your knowledge of American history vocabulary. For each definition below, choose the appropriate word or phrase from the box. You will not use all the words.

colonists	nullify	revenue-generating laws
constitutional	parliament	
negotiations	radicals	trade laws

1. Laws that raise money for a government through taxes on certain products

   _____

2. Talks between two or more groups or nations that are ready to reach an agreement

   _____

3. Rules controlling the importing and exporting of products

   _____

4. People trying to change the rules or laws of society

   _____

57

Mercy Otis Warren was an author and playwright from Massachusetts. She lived during the time of the American Revolution. Warren was critical of the British government, but she made her points through humor. Much of her work was published in Boston-area newspapers, so her ideas received a wide circulation. Warren's play *The Adulateur* was written to protest the Boston Massacre and other British acts of oppression. Through the humor in her writings, she helped make many people in Massachusetts aware of the independence movement.

58

Do you think that humor is an effective way to communicate a serious political message? Can you think of ways humor is used today to influence people's political ideas? Write one clear paragraph for your answer.

History can be seen as a long series of causes and effects. The numbered items below are some causes of the American Revolution. The lettered items below are the effects of each of these causes. Match each effect on the right with the correct cause on the left.

1. Britain needs to raise money to pay debts from the French and Indian War.

(a) Fighting breaks out at Lexington and Concord, followed soon by the Battle of Bunker Hill.

2. American colonists boycott sugar and stamps; they also practice tax evasion.

(b) Colonial leaders issue the Declaration of Independence.

3. The First Continental Congress assembles in 1774.

(c) The Intolerable Acts go into effect.

4. The Second Continental Congress assembles beginning in 1775.

(d) Britain issues the Sugar Act, Stamp Act, and Townshend Act.

5. King George issues the Proclamation of Rebellion.

(e) Colonists send the Olive Branch Petition to King George III.

59

"We have an old mother that peevish is grown;
She snubs us like children that scarce walk alone;
She forgets we're grown up and have sense of our own."

Benjamin Franklin wrote this ditty in the 1770s. What did he mean? Explain the poem in your own words.

60

Who won the battle of Bunker (Breed's) Hill? Look at the statistics below.

British troops—2,200   Continental (American) troops—3,200

British losses—1,054   Continental (American) losses—441

For each side, calculate the percentage of losses from the total number of troops.

Percentage of British losses = _____ %

Percentage of American losses = _____ %

The British won the battle in a tactical sense. However, in the words of one general, it was "a dear bought victory." What lesson do you think the British learned from this fight? Write a clear paragraph to explain your answer.

61

After the Battle of Bunker (Breed's) Hill, British General Gage wrote a letter to one of the war leaders back in England. In this letter, he said, "My Lord, you will receive an account of some success against the rebels, but attended [along] with a long list of killed and wounded on our side; so many of the latter that the hospital has hardly hands sufficient to take care of them."

Why did the British suffer such losses at Bunker Hill? Give at least three reasons.

62

In each pair of sentences below, one sentence describes a cause, and the other describes an effect. However, they are not necessarily in the right order. Indicate the cause (**C**) and the effect (**E**) for each pair of sentences.

___ 1A. The British changed their tactics in later fights to avoid unnecessary casualties.

___ 1B. British losses at the Battle of Bunker Hill were higher than colonial losses.

___ 2A. Congress, seeing that the conflict was growing, asked all able-bodied men to join the militia.

___ 2B. Citizens had to choose between the Patriot cause and the Loyalist (faithful to Britain) cause.

___ 3A. King George III refused to hear any petition from the colonists: Britain passed a new act that prohibited colonial trade and allowed American ships and sailors to be seized.

___ 3B. The Continental Congress made one last effort to make peace. The Olive Branch Petition, written in July 1775, asked the king to stop the war and repeal the Coercive Acts.

63

"I am obnoxious, suspected, and unpopular. You are much the otherwise."

Someone said this in June 1776 to Thomas Jefferson. The speaker was trying to persuade Jefferson to do something.

Who was the speaker? What did he hope Jefferson would do? Why did the speaker believe that Jefferson was the best choice for this task? Explain your answer in a clear paragraph.

64

At the start of the Revolutionary War, Britain had a number of advantages over the colonists. For example, Britain had a long tradition of skilled military servicemen. However, Britain also faced some disadvantages.

Draw a line down the center of a sheet of paper, dividing it into two columns. Label the left column *Advantages*. In it, list at least three advantages that Britain had at the start of the war. Label the right column *Disadvantages*. In it, list at least three disadvantages Britain faced.

65

© 2002 J. Weston Walch, Publisher

These words were said by General John Stark of the Continental Army before the Battle of Bennington in August 1777:

"My men, yonder are the Hessians. They were bought for seven pounds and ten pence a man. Are you worth more? Prove it. Tonight, the American flag floats from yonder hill or Molly Stark sleeps a widow!"

What is General Stark saying about the Hessians? What is he asking of his own troops? What is the meaning of the last sentence? Write a clear paragraph that answers these questions.

66

Compared with their counterparts on the British side, colonial fighters of the Revolutionary War faced two major disadvantages. The first of these was irregular, inadequate supplies. The troops could not count on a steady supply of food, clothing, and medical items. They also could not count on regular pay, because the Continental Congress could not raise money through taxes.

The second big disadvantage was a smaller number of troops. The British forces were larger (and better trained) than the colonial troops. The number of British soldiers available at any point in time was generally more predictable. In fact, the number of Continental Army soldiers fluctuated by the season.

Why did American army forces increase and decrease with the seasons? Write a clear, detailed paragraph for your answer.

67

© 2002 J. Weston Walch, Publisher

Look at the pie chart below. It shows the total number of British forces involved in the Battle of Saratoga (New York) on October 17, 1777. This was part of British General Burgoyne's plan to lead his army down from Canada into New York. He then planned to cut off the colonial fighters in New England from their fellow patriots in New York. Since the British army was much larger and more experienced, Burgoyne was quite sure his plan would work.

However, history tells a different story. Saratoga proved to be a major defeat for the British. They suffered heavy casualties, and the general had to surrender thousands of his men.

68

Half of the British forces at Saratoga were really British. Who were the other half?

Why did General Burgoyne lose this important battle? Write a clear paragraph for your answer.

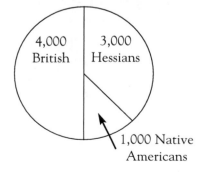

4,000 British

3,000 Hessians

1,000 Native Americans

For the Patriot side, winning the Battle of Saratoga was not just a stunning victory. It proved to be a turning point in the war. This was because the French, who had been reluctant to back the colonists at the beginning of the war, now thought that the British might lose. After Saratoga, the French agreed to form an alliance with the colonists. This had several positive effects on the colonial army.

What were the key effects of the French alliance with the colonists? List at least three effects.

69

The Revolutionary War spanned six years and involved many battles and skirmishes. Still, four events stand out in terms of importance. They are listed below. Number these battles 1 to 4 in the correct chronological order, with 1 being earliest. Then write one or two sentences to explain the historical importance of each one.

____ Valley Forge

____ Yorktown

____ Lexington and Concord

____ Saratoga

70

Read the following descriptions of British generals of the Revolutionary War. Then write the name of the appropriate general in the blank after each description.

Burgoyne	Carleton	Cornwallis	Gage	Howe

1. I was defeated by George Washington at the Battle of Princeton in 1777. _____

2. I defeated George Washington and other officers at the Battle of Brandywine in 1777. _____

3. After taking back Fort Ticonderoga earlier in the year, I surrendered my troops at the Battle of Saratoga. _____

4. I ordered my troops to Lexington and Concord in 1775 to get rid of the colonists' stockpiled weapons. _____

5. I held off colonial troops who were attacking Quebec in 1776; this is known as the Battle for Canada. _____

71

Six important Europeans are listed below. Each of these men contributed to the American cause during the war, especially with military training and advice on strategy.

In the blank after each name, write the name of the country this adviser came from.

1. Comte de Grasse _____

2. Friedrich von Steuben _____

3. Johann de Kalb _____

    4. Marquis de Lafayette _____

    5. Casimir Pulaski _____

    6. Tadeusz Kościuszko _____

72

After the Revolutionary War, the new American government could not pay its debts. War is expensive. The Second Continental Congress had borrowed money from wealthy people and other nations to pay its bills. It had also printed "Continental dollars" to pay for some things, promising to replace those dollars with silver or gold coins after the war.

The Congress asked individual states to voluntarily donate money to help pay the country's debts. However, these contributions did not add up to much. As a result, the Continental money was devalued. This led to inflation. Shortly after the war, it took 40 Continental dollars to equal one gold dollar.

Why did the new nation's economic problems persuade many people—especially rich ones—that the government needed more legal powers? Why were the Articles of Confederation not working well enough? Explain your answer in one clear paragraph.

73

The Articles of Confederation were

established by the Second Continental Congress in 1777. They provided a design and structure for the new American government.

Which of the following did the Articles of Confederation allow the government to do? Put a check mark next to each item below that was allowed. Of the things that the government was *not* allowed to do, which do you think was the most needed? Write a clear paragraph explaining your answer.

74

___ Fight wars

___ Form armies

___ Enforce its laws

___ Control trade between states

___ Print and borrow money

___ Make decisions about Native Americans

___ Establish a postal service

___ Control trade with other nations

___ Establish and collect taxes

For each definition below, choose the appropriate word from the box.

confederation	legislature	ratify
constitution	plurality	simple majority

1. An elected group of representatives who make laws on behalf of the people _____

2. To formally agree to a new plan or law, often by voting _____

3. A written plan for the government of a country _____

4. Half of a group, plus one _____

5. More of something (like votes) than anyone else gets, but not more than half of the total number cast; applies to groups of more than two _____

6. An alliance or league _____

75

The Constitution of the United States of America was written to make the central government of the new country stronger than it had been under the Articles of Confederation.

Here is the preamble to the Constitution of the United States:

We the people of the United States, in order to form a more perfect union, establish justice, ensure domestic tranquility, provide for the common defense, promote the general welfare, and secure the blessings of liberty to ourselves and our posterity, do ordain and establish this Constitution for the United States of America.

In the preamble above, underline the six goals that the writers had in mind for the Constitution.

76

Which of these goals do you think is the most important? Why? Explain your answer in a clear paragraph. Support it with examples.

For each definition below, choose the appropriate word or phrase from the box. Not all the words in the box will be used.

amendment	article	clause	perjury
appropriate	civic	federal	precedent

1. A formal, written change—for example, to the Constitution _____

2. Something that sets an example for later decision makers _____

3. National _____

4. To set aside money for a special purpose _____

77

Each definition below relates to the United States Congress in some way. Choose the word or phrase from the box that fits each definition best. Not all the words in the box will be used.

commerce	joint committee
constituents	legislation
election	standing committee
intelligence committee	tax law

78

1. People who have elected someone to government _____

2. Permanent committee in the House or Senate _____

3. A committee made up of members of both houses of Congress _____

4. The process of making laws _____

5. Business on a large scale _____

At the Constitutional Convention of 1787,

there was much arguing over how many votes each state should get in the House of Representatives. It was decided that each state would be given a certain number of votes based on its population; the larger the population, the more votes in Congress. One area of disagreement was whether slaves should count as part of a state's population. There was also controversy over property taxes: Should slaves count as property or not?

How did the North and South differ on this subject? Describe the hypocrisy shown by the Southern members of Congress on the issue of how slaves should be counted. (Look up the word *hypocrisy* in a dictionary if you need help.) Write a clear paragraph explaining your answer.

79

Fill in the chart below by writing "yes" or "no" as appropriate, based on the situation in America in 1787 at the time of the Constitutional Convention.

Based on the completed chart, what major differences were there between North and South in 1787? Where will these differences lead in the nineteenth century? Write one or two sentences for your answer.

80

	Economy based on slavery?	Large slave population?	Wants slaves to count as property for taxes?	Wants slaves to count as votes in Congress?
North				
South				

Three major compromises were made at the Constitutional Convention in 1787. Describe each one in two to three sentences.

81

For each definition related to American government listed below, provide an appropriate vocabulary word.

1. Each side gives in a little to find a common solution or agreement. _____

2. A law that Congress drafts and wants to pass _____

3. The president rejects or cancels a bill from Congress. _____

4. Branch of government with the power to make laws _____

5. Branch of government with the power to enforce laws _____

6. Branch of government with the power to interpret and rule on laws _____

7. Congress passes a bill in spite of the president's veto. _____

8. To formally charge a public official with breaking a law _____

82

Freedom of speech is constitutionally protected in the United States Bill of Rights. Which amendment covers freedom of speech?

_____

In reality, free speech has often become the subject of court cases. Should there be some limits to free speech? Can there be such a thing as too much freedom of speech—for example, speaking out against the government in a time of national crisis? Could there be times when free speech does more harm than good? Write a clear paragraph explaining your opinion.

83

© 2002 J. Weston Walch, Publisher

The United States court system is based on the assumption that defendants are innocent until they are proven guilty. The Constitution provides for a fair and speedy trial for all defendants. The system allows for verdicts to be appealed.

Write a definition for each court-related word or phrase below. You may need to use a dictionary for some of the terms.

1. attorney

2. bail

3. civil case

4. criminal case

5. double jeopardy

Each term below relates to the American court system. Write a definition for each word or phrase. You may need to use a dictionary in some cases.

1. defendant

2. grand jury

3. probable cause

4. search warrant

5. subpoena

85

The First Lady has no clear job that is defined by the government. However, First Ladies have traditionally served the public in many ways—for example, in matters involving health, education, historic preservation, or the environment. Martha Washington, the first First Lady, helped veterans of the Revolutionary War. She also served as hostess at many formal teas and dinners at the presidential residence. Martha Washington believed that it was important to impress foreign guests so that they would take her country and her husband—the nation's first president—seriously.

86

Do you think this is still important today? Should our government leaders continue to try to impress foreign dignitaries? Does this require a relatively formal approach? Write a clear paragraph explaining your answer. Support your opinion with examples from history and current events.

At many times in American history, citizens have protested against laws or practices that they consider unfair. Two such examples are the protests made against the Stamp Act of 1765 and the Whiskey Tax of 1794.

Compare and contrast these two events. Who protested in each case? To whom did they protest? What were their arguments against these taxes? What forms of protest did they choose to use? Write a clear paragraph for your answer. Be as specific as possible.

87

Supporters of Thomas Jefferson sang the
following verse in 1798, to the tune of "Yankee Doodle Dandy":

> See Johnny at the helm of State,
> Head itching for a crowny,
> He longs to be, like Georgy, great
> And pull Tom Jeffer downy.

Who is "Johnny"?

Who is "Georgy"?

What is the song implying about these two men? Write one or two
sentences to explain your answer.

88

At the end of the eighteenth century, America had a conflict with France. It led to what is known as the XYZ Affair. This experience led Congress to pass laws placing tighter restrictions on foreigners in the United States. The terms below relate to this period. Write a definition for each term. You may need to use your textbook or another resource to provide some of the definitions.

1. alien
2. deadlock
3. judicial review

4. laissez-faire
5. sedition
6. unconstitutional

89

George Washington's country home was at Mount Vernon, Virginia. In it, there is a key to the Bastille—the infamous French prison of the eighteenth century. The French general Lafayette gave the key to Washington in 1790.

Why did Lafayette give Washington this key? Write your answer in a clear paragraph. It should include an explanation of the relationship between France and colonial America.

90

What foreign policy advice did George Washington give the country in his farewell address? Explain in one or two sentences.

_____

There is a word for this kind of policy toward other countries. What is it? _____

Do you agree or disagree with Washington's advice? Was it a good idea for America at the time? Is it a good idea now? Write a clear paragraph that explains your answer. Support your opinion with examples.

91

Thomas Jefferson wrote his own epitaph before he died. These words appear at his grave at Monticello, his beloved Virginia home:

> Here was buried
> Thomas Jefferson
> Author of the Declaration of American Independence
> Of the Statute of Virginia for Religious Freedom and
> Father of the University of Virginia.

Jefferson left out some of his most important accomplishments. Name two achievements of Jefferson's that could easily have been added. Why do you think he left them out? Write one or two sentences to explain your answer.

92

Thomas Jefferson was the American ambassador to France from 1784 to 1789. While abroad, he studied architecture. He took special notice of the many classical ruins in Rome and other parts of Italy. Jefferson was so influenced by what he saw that he introduced the "classical style" to America when he returned.

Think of some examples of buildings that show the classical style. They could be national landmarks, or buildings in your community. What special features make these buildings "classical"? Write a paragraph describing these features. Make a sketch of one building to show your class.

93

© 2002 J. Weston Walch, Publisher

"Educate and inform the whole mass of the people."

Thomas Jefferson gave this advice to James Madison, Jefferson's successor as president.

Do you think that Jefferson's advice is good? What might happen if all of a country's people are not educated and informed? Does the United States do a good job of educating the "whole mass of the people"? Write a clear paragraph that supports your answer to the question.

94

Four U.S. presidents were referred to as the "Virginia Planter" presidents. Who were they? Why were they called this? Write your answers below. Then check them with a classmate.

95

In 1804, a Shawnee Indian named the Prophet (Tenskwatawa) had a vision. In this vision, the people from his tribe had given up all the customs introduced by white men. The Prophet urged the Shawnee to stop trading in white goods, to avoid liquor, and to go back to their old ways. This would give them back the power they had lost to the white culture. It would allow them to resist the white invasions. In 1808, the Prophet settled along Tippecanoe Creek with a band of followers.

What happened at Tippecanoe Creek just seven years later? Why was the Prophet's vision not achieved in the end? Write a clear paragraph explaining your answer.

96

The Prophet's older brother, Tecumseh, organized thousands of Native Americans into a confederation. In 1810, he sent a message to William Henry Harrison, who was governor of Indiana Territory at the time. Tecumseh said that the land belonged to all of the Indians and could not be sold by any one Indian leader. If the entire nation of Native Americans did not agree, the deal was not valid. He formally protested the government's attempts to drive the native peoples from their land. His protests were not successful.

What role did Tecumseh play just a few years later, during the War of 1812? Do you think he was justified in taking on this role? Write a clear paragraph, giving reasons for your answer.

97

During the War of 1812, Britain blockaded the United States by sea. This was meant to cause hardship for America. In fact, the blockade ended up doing the country a favor.

Write a clear paragraph explaining why the British blockade actually helped the United States in the long run. Support your answer with examples from history.

98

The War of 1812 was the first war fought by the newly formed United States of America. Decide whether each statement below describes a cause of the War of 1812, or an effect. Write **C** (cause) or **E** (effect) on the line beside each statement.

_____ 1. The party of wealthy business people (the Federalist Party) became unpopular. It eventually came to an end.

_____ 2. Britain supported and armed Native Americans to fight against the Americans.

_____ 3. The British attacked American ships that were trying to trade with France.

_____ 4. Native Americans could no longer gather together effectively to fight the U.S. government.

_____ 5. Domestic manufacturing increased and imports decreased.

_____ 6. Britain boarded American trading ships and forced sailors to join the British navy.

_____ 7. Some prominent Americans wanted to add Canada and Florida to the United States.

99

An important event took place in September 1813.
This popular song was written to commemorate it:

> The tenth of September
> Let us all remember,
> As long as the world on its axis goes round;
> Our tars and marines
> On Lake Erie were seen
> To make the proud flag of Great Britain come down.

What event does the song commemorate? Why was the event so important? Write a clear paragraph explaining your answer.

100

Andrew Jackson was given many nicknames during his long military and political career.

Name at least two of his nicknames. Write a sentence explaining why he was given that name.

One of his nicknames was "the Hero of New Orleans." Write one or two sentences explaining why he was given that name.

101

Andrew Jackson's official presidential cabinet (group of advisers) had six members. However, he also assembled an informal group of about a dozen advisers who gave him help as needed. The press began calling this group his "Lower Cabinet" or "Kitchen Cabinet." Many presidents since Jackson have used groups like this.

Do you approve or disapprove of this concept? What might be some advantages and/or disadvantages of an informal group like this advising the president? Write a clear paragraph explaining your answer. Support your opinion with examples.

In 1827, a newspaper man named James Webb of the *New York Courier* had an idea. He started collecting news and selling it to other newspapers in town as a convenience. Henry Raymond of Boston later expanded this concept, selling Boston news to New York newspapers. This eventually led to the birth of the Associated Press (AP) on January 11, 1849. This was a cooperative organization that collected and distributed news to the daily press.

Does this type of organization still exist today? What are the advantages and disadvantages of this type of news organization? Write two or three sentences to explain your answer.

105

Innovations in technology have been *vital* to the development of the American nation. Match each invention on the left with the *name* of the person credited with its creation, on the right.

Inventions

1. conestoa wagon (1750)

2. lightnin rod (1753)

3. automat flour mill (1785)

4. cotton g (1793)

5. steam locmotive (1830)

6. steel plow1837)

7. sewing maine (1843)

8. horse-drawmechanical reaper (184

Inventors

(a) John Deere (Midwest)

(b) Peter Cooper (Maryland)

(c) Oliver Evans (Maryland)

(d) Elias Howe (Massachusetts)

(e) Eli Whitney (Connecticut)

(f) Cyrus McCormick (Illinois)

(g) Benjamin Franklin (Pennsylvania)

(h) German craftsmen (Pennsylvania)

Below is a list of unusual phrases that were introduced to American English during the Industrial Revolution. Write a definition for each term. You may need to consult a dictionary or textbook for some of them.

1. canal boy

2. floating palace

3. Lowell girl

4. corduroy road

5. spinning jenny

107

© 2002 J. Weston Walch, Publisher

The following poem is called the "Song of the Manchester Factory Girl."

She tends the loom, she watches the spindle,
  And cheerfully talketh away;
Mid the din of wheels, how her bright eyes kindle!
  And her [heart] is ever gay.

Do you think that this is an accurate picture of factory life for a young woman in the early nineteenth century? Write a clear paragraph explaining your answer. Support your answer with some examples from history.

108

In 1837, two American sisters, Angelina and Sarah Grimké, began a lecture tour to promote the abolitionist movement. It was unusual enough for two sisters to speak publicly at that time in American history. However, their family circumstances made it even more unusual: They were from an aristocratic, slave-owning South Carolina family. The two women had come to hate the cruelty and injustice of slavery. However, they were forced to do their speaking in the North only—their criticisms would not have been tolerated at home. Even in the North, they were accused of being "unnatural." As well-bred young ladies, they should not have been willing to talk publicly about the horrors of slavery and the plight of women in American society.

The Grimké sisters showed great courage. They broke with their Southern traditions and culture for a cause they cared deeply about. Can you think of other examples from American history where someone has spoken out for a cause despite real personal risk? Name at least two people, and the causes they spoke up for.

109

In 1840, General William Henry ("Tippecanoe") Harrison of Ohio ran for president against Martin Van Buren. A newspaper critic once said of Harrison, "Give him a barrel of hard cider, and settle a pension of $2,000 a year on him, and . . . he will sit the remainder of his days in his log cabin. . . ." This implied that Harrison was a poor, lazy bumpkin who drank hard (alcoholic) cider instead of "refined" drinks. The critic was suggesting that Harrison wouldn't amount to much.

This statement was meant to criticize Harrison. However, it actually did just the reverse—it started a myth. Suddenly, Harrison was known as a down-to-earth, honest "man of the people." Farmers and other less wealthy Americans decided to vote for him. Harrison won the election.

Interestingly, Harrison was not at all poor or simple. He was from a wealthy Virginia family. He had been to college and now lived in a mansion.

Compare what you have just learned about the campaign of 1840 with political campaigns today. Do you see any similarities? What part do the media play in distorting or trivializing the candidates and/or the issues? Write a clear paragraph explaining your answer. Try to give some examples from contemporary political life.

The following song is titled "Get Off the Track." It was written during a presidential election.

> Railroads to Emancipation
> Cannot rest on Clay foundation.
> And the road that Polk erects us
> Leads to slavery and to Texas!

Which election do you think this song is referring to? What are the main points this song makes about each of the two candidates? Write a clear paragraph explaining your answer.

111

In 1848, the first woman's rights convention was held at Seneca Falls, New York. Members of the group composed a Declaration of Sentiments. This declaration was similar in phrasing and style to the Declaration of Independence. Here is part of the Declaration from Seneca: "The history of mankind is a history of repeated injuries and usurpations on the part of man toward woman."

Rewrite the quotation above using your own words. Then, in a clear paragraph, tell whether you agree or disagree with the statement. Support your response with examples from history.

Why do you think the writers of the Seneca Declaration used phrasing that was similar to that in the Declaration of Independence?

112

The pie chart below shows a breakdown of the total number of immigrants who came to the United States between 1840 and 1849, as reported in the 1850 census.

▨ Irish
▨ German
▨ British Isles
■ Other

Immigrants by Country of Origin, 1840–1849

Who made up the largest group of immigrants during the decade reflected here? _____

Why was this the largest group? What factors at home may have driven them to come to America? Write two or three sentences explaining your answer.

113

© 2002 J. Weston Walch, Publisher

In the middle of the nineteenth century, the United States government tried to acquire Cuba from Spain—both peacefully and by force. Their efforts were unsuccessful.

Why did the United States want to add Cuba to its territory? Name at least two reasons.

114

Uncle Tom's Cabin; or, *Life Among the Lowly* was published in 1852. It was read by hundreds of thousands of people in the United States—especially in the North—and abroad. This book told a dramatic story about slave life on a Southern plantation. It proved to be a powerful abolitionist tool, helping to persuade many people that slavery was wrong and should be ended in America. Some Southerners called the book's author, Harriet Beecher Stowe, "the vile wretch in petticoats."

Why do you think *Uncle Tom's Cabin*—a novel—made such an impact? Think of other works of literature that have influenced people politically. Name at least one example.

115

"No man is good enough to govern another man without that other's consent."

—Abraham Lincoln, 1854
(speaking for the newly-formed Republican Party)

To what do you think Lincoln is referring? Be sure to consider the date of this statement. What particular group of people do you think he was most concerned about? Can you think of some other examples from U.S. history of certain individuals being governed without their consent? Write your answer in two or three sentences.

116

At the beginning of the Civil War, General Winfield Scott predicted that the North would win the war, but that it would take three years. He also predicted that the Union would encircle the South and squeeze it to death like a giant anaconda snake. Many people laughed at this and joked about "Scott's anaconda."

Did Scott's predictions come true? Was the anaconda analogy an appropriate one? Write a clear paragraph explaining your answer. Support it with details from Civil War history.

117

© 2002 J. Weston Walch, Publisher

Around the middle of the nineteenth century, the United States government gave millions of acres of land in the West to two large corporations. This was done so that the transcontinental railroad could be built.

Was this transaction fair? What do you think the advantages and disadvantages of this arrangement may have been? Draw a line down the center of a sheet of paper, dividing it into two columns. List advantages in the left column. List disadvantages in the right column.

118

Do governments in this country (either local, state, or federal) still make special arrangements with businesses from time to time? Perhaps you can think of some examples from your own community. In these cases, do the advantages outweigh the disadvantages? Explain your answer in a paragraph.

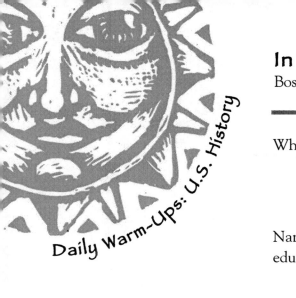

In the middle of the nineteenth century, the city of Boston was sometimes called the "Athens of America."

Why did Boston have this nickname?

Name at least three reasons for this nickname. Consider politics, education, and literature in your answer.

119

© 2002 J. Weston Walch, Publisher

There were three candidates for president in the election of 1856. The Democratic candidate was James Buchanan. He won the election. The Republican candidate was John Fremont. The Know-Nothing party candidate was Millard Fillmore. He got the least number of votes.

How did the Know-Nothing party get its name? Write one sentence to explain your answer.

120

The Know-Nothings were white Protestants who were antiforeign, anti-immigrant, and anti-Catholic. They promoted something called *nativism*. What was this? Write one sentence to explain your anwer.

How does the concept of patriotism compare with that of nativism? Which do you think is preferable? Explain your reasoning in one clear paragraph.

When the United States Supreme Court decided against Dred Scott in 1857, many Americans were shocked and angry. They said the Southern justices on the Court were influenced by racism and a proslavery bias. Some critics said that the justices had "sullied the ermine."

What do you think the expression "sullied the ermine" means here? Write a clear paragraph to explain your answer.

Can you think of any more recent cases from history in which the U.S. Supreme Court has been accused by many citizens of bias in making its decision?

121

© 2002 J. Weston Walch, Publisher

"A house divided against itself cannot stand."

—Abraham Lincoln,
at the Republican State Convention of 1858

What was Lincoln referring to in this statement? Why do you think Lincoln used the metaphor of a house to make his point? Explain your answer in one clear paragraph.

122

When the United States Census Bureau issued its 1860 report, it included "civilized Indians" in the statistics.

What do you think the word *civilized* means here? Do you think that American Indians would agree with this use of the word as applied to their condition in 1860? Write a clear paragraph explaining your answer. Support your opinion with some examples from history.

123

When visitors go to the United States Capitol building, they are given a self-guided tour booklet. It includes the following passage:

> A crypt is commonly acknowledged as an underground vault or burial chamber, although there is no one buried in the Capitol. The original intent was to inter [bury] the remains of _____ under the center of this room.

Who do you think was meant to be buried at the Capitol? Why? Write down the reasons for your choice.

124

Robert C. Winthrop made this remark in Boston in 1862:

> "Let us keep our eyes and our hearts steadily fixed upon the old flag of our fathers. . . . It has a star for every state. Let us resolve that there shall be a state for every star!"

How many states were in the Union in 1862? _____

How many states were in the Confederacy? _____

What is Winthrop urging? Write two or three sentences to explain your answer.

125

Use the chart below to organize the important Civil War battles and events listed in the box. The number of bullets in each column indicates how many events should be listed for that particular year.

Battle of Antietam	Battle of Fort Morgan (Mobile)	Emancipation Proclamation
First Battle of Bull Run	Battle of Fredericksburg	Gettysburg Address
Battle of Chattanooga	Battle of Shiloh	Second Battle of Bull Run
Battle of Five Forks		Siege of Vicksburg

126

1861	1862	1863	1864	1865
•	•	•	•	•
	•	•		
	•	•		
	•	•		

The following passage is part of the life story of a former slave named Solomon Northup. He had been enslaved on a cotton plantation in Louisiana in the 1840s.

An hour before daylight the horn is blown. Then the slaves arouse, prepare their breakfast, fill a gourd with water, in another deposit their dinner of cold bacon and corn cake, and hurry to the field again. It is an offense invariably followed by a flogging to be found at the quarters after daybreak. Then the fears and labors of another day begin; until its close there is no such thing as rest. He fears he will be caught lagging through the day; he fears to approach the gin house with his basket-load of cotton at night; he fears, when he lies down, that he will oversleep himself in the mornings. . . .

(Solomon Northup, "Picking Cotton." Milton Meltzer, ed.
A History in Their Own Words: The Black Americans, Crowell, 1987)

List all the things Northup fears. Why does he fear these things?
Explain your answer in two or three sentences.

Imagine you are a slave with Northrup. Write a paragraph describing your life.

127

In 1860, 5 of the 10 richest states in the United States were southern: South Carolina, Georgia, Mississippi, Louisiana, and Texas. In 1880, 0 out of 10—in fact, 0 out of 20—of the richest states were southern.

Why do you think this was the case? List at least three specific causes.

128

The Homestead Act of 1862 was designed to settle the western United States beyond the Great Plains. Under this act, a farmer could have 160 acres of land for free after living on it for five years. Or, after six months on the land, he could buy it at $1.25 an acre. The law was meant to benefit small farmers and urban workers. Only one out of every nine acres of western land actually ended up in the hands of small farmers. Western land did not prove to be as easy to cultivate as land in the east.

Who ended up owning the land? Why? Name at least three reasons small farmers found it hard to settle the West.

129

Look at the graph below. It shows how many miles of railroad track had been laid in the United States at two different times.

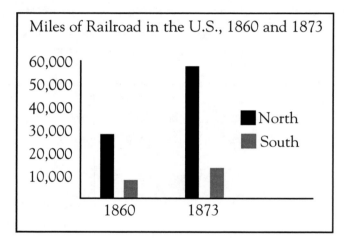

Miles of Railroad in the U.S., 1860 and 1873

60,000
50,000
40,000
30,000
20,000
10,000

1860   1873

■ North
■ South

130

What key event happened between 1860 and 1873? _____

How did this affect railroad development in different parts of the United States? Write a clear paragraph for your answer. Be as specific as possible.

Draw a line to connect each law in the left column with the corresponding description on the right.

1. Homestead Act (1862)

2. Desert Land Act (1877)

3. Timber and Stone Act (1878)

(a) This law granted 160 acres of forested land in the Northwest for $2.50. Timber magnates used deceptive methods to acquire about 3.6 million of those acres.

(b) Once the U.S. government had forced most of the Navaho and Apache peoples onto reservations, it offered to rent dry western land at 25 cents per acre if the settlers irrigated it.

(c) To draw settlers to the Great Plains and into the Northwest, this act allowed them to buy 160 acres for $1.25 per acre. They could have 160 acres for free if they lived on the land and farmed it for five years.

131

Match each major event or legislative change on the left with the appropriate name on the right.

1. It settled 80,000 former slaves on land in Georgia and South Carolina and set up schools and hospitals for them. _____

2. This amendment to the Constitution gave U.S. citizenship to all people born or naturalized in the U.S. _____

3. This act gave black Americans citizenship and equal protection under the law. President Johnson vetoed the act. Congress overrode the veto and the act became law in 1866. _____

4. This constitutional amendment gave black males the right to vote. _____

5. This amendment to the Constitution made all forms of slavery illegal. _____

(a) the Freedmen's Bureau

(b) Civil Rights Act (1866)

(c) Thirteenth Amendment (1865)

(d) Fourteenth Amendment (1866)

(e) Fifteenth Amendment (1869)

132

After the Civil War, Congress set up a program called Reconstruction. This was meant to revive the South. The changes made during Reconstruction improved life for African Americans. They were given some rights that they had not had before.

Reconstruction ended in 1877. Even before then, though, less northern attention was being paid to Reconstruction efforts in the South. The North faced a serious economic crisis: the Panic of 1873. This crisis brought on a depression that lasted for five years.

How did the depression of the 1870s affect northern Reconstructionists and southern African Americans? Write a clear paragraph explaining your answer. Be as specific as possible.

133

© 2002 J. Weston Walch, Publisher

Three American Indian tribes and their outcomes are described below. Read each passage. Then fill in the blanks with the appropriate name from the box.

Apache	Navajo	Cheyenne

1. The _____ settled on a large reservation on some of their old land in Arizona and New Mexico. The government wanted silver and copper veins in the area. Unlike most other tribes, these farmers and sheepherders could continue this work on the reservation.

2. The _____ lived by hunting and raiding. They fought the white invaders until 1870, when Chief Cochise signed a treaty placing the tribe on a reservation. Others conducted more raids on white settlements under their leader, Geronimo.

3. The _____ lived in Colorado. Their land was attractive to gold prospectors and settlers. The tribe resisted. The Colorado military sent troops out to put an end to the group, who were living at Sand Creek. The soldiers killed hundreds of American Indians there in 1864—including Chief Black Kettle.

Between 1869 and 1875, more than 200 major battles were fought between U.S. government forces and various American Indian tribes.

Why was there so much fighting during this period? What political, social, and economic factors increased the friction between American Indians and white Americans? Explain your answer in one clear paragraph.

135

© 2002 J. Weston Walch, Publisher

The second half of the nineteenth century was an era of westward expansion. During this time, many Mexican Americans and Native Americans were caught in the government's grab for land for white settlement and development.

What happened to these two groups? Explain. Copy the chart below on another sheet of paper and fill in as much information as possible. You may need to use resource materials to answer some of the questions.

	Mexican Americans	Native Americans
Did they get to keep their homes and land?		
Did they resist the U.S. government?		
Was employment available in the areas where they ended up living?		
Was there any assimilation (mixing in) with the newly-arrived white culture?		

136

After the Civil War, manufacturing centers of the North grew quickly. The last third of the nineteenth century saw a boom in northern industry. It also saw a trend toward regional economies. Different industries grew in different areas. Soon, there were two separate economies in the North.

1. What were the two geographical regions in the northern economy?

_____   _____

2. What geographical feature divided them? _____

3. Which types of commerce did each region specialize in?

_____

137

© 2002 J. Weston Walch, Publisher

Some inventions of the Industrial Revolution affected the farms of the American Midwest. For example, the McCormick reaper cut harvest work from three days to three hours. Still, not all aspects of farm life were improved by these technological advances. Read the passage below about life in 1874.

> Although a constantly improving collection of farm machinery lightened the burdens of the husbandman [farmer], the drudgery of the housewife's dishwashing and cooking did not correspondingly lessen. I fear it increased, for with the widening of the fields came the doubling of the harvest hands, and my mother continued to do most of the housework herself—cooking, sewing, washing, churning, and nursing the sick from time to time. . . . the round of Mother's duties must have been as relentless as a treadmill.
>
> (Hamlin Garland, *A Son of the Middle Border,* 1917)

138

How did improvements in farm machinery affect the farmer? How did those changes affect the farmer's wife? What skills did a farming housewife need at that time?

American history is filled with tales of exploration, settlement, conflict, and technological innovation. Little is usually said about the role of the women who supported these efforts. Why? Write a clear paragraph for your answer.

© 2002 J. Weston Walch, Publisher

Jacob A. Riis was a Danish immigrant. He became a newspaper reporter in New York City at the end of the nineteenth century. Riis wanted to draw attention to the poverty and unhealthy living conditions in the city's tenements. Here is an extract from Riis's famous work, *How the Other Half Lives*. This book had a great effect on the reform movement of that era.

Be a little careful, please! The hall is dark, and you might stumble over the children pitching pennies back there . . . . A flight of stairs. You can feel your way if you cannot see it. Close [stuffy]? Yes! . . . . All the fresh air that ever enters these stairs comes from the hall door that is forever slamming . . . . The sinks are in the hallway, that all the tenants may have access— and all be poisoned alike by their summer stenches. . . . In summer, when a thousand thirsty throats pant for a cooling drink in this block, [the pump] is worked in vain. . . . Listen! That short, hacking cough, that tiny, helpless wail—what do they mean? . . . The child is dying of measles. With half a chance it might have lived, but it had none. That dark bedroom killed it.

Who are "the other half"? _____

Riis was a newspaper reporter. Do news reporters today still work to draw attention to problems in society? Explain your answer in a paragraph.

139

© 2002 J. Weston Walch, Publisher

America is often called the country of immigrants. Some come to the United States for political or religious freedom. Others seek the "American dream" of prosperity. Life in America could be confusing for new immigrants. This passage describes the experience of a young woman from Russia.

> A committee of our friends . . . put their heads together and concocted American names for us all. Those of our real names that had no pleasing American equivalents they ruthlessly discarded. . . . My mother, possessing a name that was not easily translatable, was punished with the undignified nickname of Annie. Fetchke, Joseph, and Deborah issued as Frieda, Joseph, and Dora, respectively.
>
> (Mary Antin, *The Promised Land*, 1912)

140

Officials at Ellis Island changed the names of many immigrants. Why? Do you think this was appropriate? Explain your answer in one clear paragraph.

Imagine that the government has officially changed your name. How do you feel? Write one or two paragraphs describing how this affects you.

John D. Rockefeller was an American industrialist who made a fortune in the late nineteenth century. He once made the following comments:

> I say that you ought to get rich, and it is your duty to get rich . . . . Ninety-eight out of one hundred of the rich men of America are honest. That is why they are rich. That is why they are trusted with money. That is why they carry on great enterprises and find plenty of people to work with them. . . . I sympathize with the poor, but the number of poor who are to be sympathized with is very small . . . let us remember there is not a poor person in the United States who was not made poor by his own shortcomings.

What does Rockefeller seem to think about people who have money? What does he think of people who do not have money? Explain your answer in one or two sentences.

How do you think a manual laborer, factory worker, or office clerk might react to these statements? Respond to the thoughts expressed in each sentence of the quotation. Write your answer in a clear paragraph.

141

In the late 1800s, Congress passed laws designed to limit the power of monopolies and "clean up" government. Much of this legislation was ineffective.

Match each law described on the left with its name on the right.

1. This act made the railroads charge "reasonable and just rates" to businesses needing transportation for their products. _____

2. This act made it illegal for companies to form trusts or prevent competition. However, this was hard to enforce. Many cases ended up in court. _____

3. This act controlled how some government jobs were filled. The Civil Service Exam was set up to keep people from being appointed to jobs by their friends and relatives. _____

(a) Pendleton Act (1883)

(b) Interstate Commerce Act (1887)

(c) Sherman Antitrust Act (1890)

142

What do all of the following companies have in common?

Standard Oil Company   American Tobacco Company

Northern Securities Corporation   Bell Telephone Company

Armour Company

When were they started? How did they become strong? What was
their effect on American businesses at the time? What did each
business specialize in? (Some will be easy to identify!) Write your
answer in one clear paragraph.

143

Draw a line from each event from American labor history on the left to its date on the right.

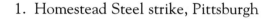

1. Homestead Steel strike, Pittsburgh

2. Pullman strike, Chicago

3. Founding of the Knights of Labor

4. Founding of the American Federation of Labor (AFL)

5. Founding of Industrial Workers of the World (IWW)

6. Pittsburgh Rail strike

(a) 1869

(b) 1886

(c) 1877

(d) 1892

(e) 1894

(f) 1905

144

Around 1900, child labor was often used in American factories and farms. At the turn of the century, nearly one million children under the age of fifteen were working for American industries. Another million worked on farms. This led to abuses and serious safety issues. About a decade later, people began to protest for better child labor laws.

What are the child labor laws in your state today? Depending on their age, are children limited to certain kinds of jobs? Are the hours they can work each week limited? Do you think these laws are good? Write a clear paragraph explaining your answer.

145

© 2002 J. Weston Walch, Publisher

There were two serious economic downturns in America at the end of the nineteenth century. One was the depression of 1873. The other was the depression of 1893. During the 1893 crisis, 20 percent of American workers lost their jobs; 17 percent of American railroads failed. Both of these depressions were caused by similar economic conditions.

What conditions caused both depressions? How did the depression of 1873 and the depression of 1893 affect the number of monopolies in the United States? Write two or three sentences to explain your answer.

146

At the end of the nineteenth century, American farmers and poor urban workers faced many problems. The Populist party was formed in response to those problems. In 1892, the Populists ran a candidate for president. Here is part of the party platform:

> The people are demoralized . . . . The newspapers are largely subsidized or muzzled, public opinion silenced, business prostrated, homes covered with mortgages, labor impoverished, and the land concentrating in the hands of capitalists. . . . The fruits of the toil of millions are boldly stolen to build up the colossal fortunes for a few, unprecedented in the history of mankind; and the possessors of these in turn despise the Republic and endanger liberty. From the same prolific womb of governmental injustice we breed the two great classes—tramps and millionaires. . . .

Does this excerpt describe a healthy democracy? Write one clear paragraph explaining your answer.

The Populist platform mentioned two classes of people in America. Who were they? To which class do you think most Populists would have said they belonged?

147

© 2002 J. Weston Walch, Publisher

At the turn of the twentieth century, two foreign powers had navies that were larger than that of the United States. Who were they? _____   _____

President Theodore Roosevelt wanted to increase the size of the U.S. navy. Why? Write one clear paragraph explaining your answer. Be as detailed as possible.

148

In the early 1900s, the United States wanted to expand. It was looking for new trading partners, new supplies of natural resources, and new land—especially in the Pacific and the Caribbean.

Draw a line from each Caribbean location on the left to the appropriate historic event on the right.

1. Cuba

2. Dominican Republic

3. Puerto Rico

(a) Spain gave this island to the United States in 1898.

(b) The U.S. still leases a naval base at Guantánamo Bay on this island.

(c) In 1905, the U.S. sent troops to this country. The troops stayed there until 1924.

149

Match each word in the box to the correct definition.

accommodation	imperialism
diplomacy	nationalism
domination	

1. A powerful nation controls a weaker one. It keeps citizens of the weaker country from making their own political or economic decisions. _____

2. A sense of loyalty to one's country; the feeling that one's country is better than others _____

3. Communicating regularly with another country to ensure good relations _____

4. One country uses its greater power to control another country. _____

5. One government adjusts its approach to another country because both countries seem to have equal power. _____

150

The following graphs show the three largest cities in the United States at two different points in time: 1820 and 1900.

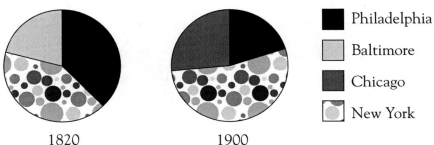

1820   1900

■ Philadelphia

▨ Baltimore

▨ Chicago

⊙ New York

1. Which cities can be found in both graphs? Has anything changed about their relative order? Write one or two sentences to explain your answer.

2. Which city appears in 1820 but not in 1900? Which city appears in 1900 but not 1820? Can you think of any reason for this? Write two or three sentences to explain your answer.

3. What other observations can you make based on these graphs? Write two or three sentences to explain your answer.

151

Just before World War I, about one third of all Americans were first- or second-generation immigrants. When the war broke out in Europe, many of these American citizens still felt very close to their "old countries."

Which ethnic groups in the United States might have favored the nations of the Central Powers? Why? Write one or two sentences to explain your answer.

Which ethnic groups might have favored the Allies? Why? Write one or two sentences to explain your answer.

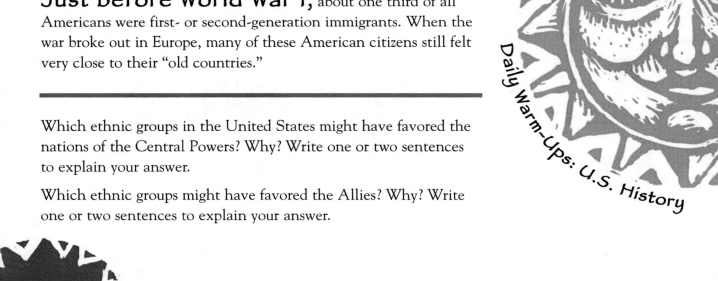

152

On March 1, 1917, the text of a telegram was published in American newspapers. It was called the Zimmerman Telegram. This telegram made many readers angry. It helped make people more willing to consider war with Germany and the other Central Powers.

Who wrote the Zimmerman Telegram? To whom was it addressed? What was the basic message of the telegram? What was the motive of the person (or nation) sending this message? Write one clear paragraph to explain your answer.

153

The United States joined World War I in 1917. This helped turn the tide of the war in Europe.

All the events below took place in 1918 and involved American troops. Number them 1 to 5 in chronological order.

____ (a) Saint Mihiel offensive (France)—General Pershing leads as U.S. army troops overcome a German stronghold and take thousands of prisoners.

154

____ (b) Ypres-Lys offensive/Passendale (Belgium)—This unsuccessful British-led drive results in many Allied casualties.

____ (c) Aisne-Marne offensive/Second Battle of the Marne (France)—U.S. troops help keep Germans from crossing the Marne River in a turning point in the war.

____ (d) Meuse-Argonne offensive (France)—The U.S. First Army takes major German defenses; this results in armistice talks.

____ (e) Battle of Vittorio-Veneto (Italy)—This battle succeeds in driving out the Austrian army.

These three statements describe the American economy in the 1920s. For each statement, explain why this factor helped lead to the Great Depression that began with the stock market crash of 1929.

1. Many Americans in the 1920s thought prosperity would continue. They bought household appliances and cars on credit.

2. As the American economy grew in the early 1900s, it became concentrated in the hands of fewer corporations.

3. In the mid-1920s, the smallest and richest group of Americans invested heavily in high-risk ventures.

155

During the Great Depression, many people had to give up their homes because they could no longer pay the rent or the mortgage. Some ended up living on the streets. Some lived in settlements of houses made of scrap material on the fringes of cities. These areas were often called "Hoovervilles." Newspapers were sometimes called "Hoover blankets."

Why were these names used? Was it fair to blame President Hoover for the Great Depression? Write one clear paragraph to explain your answer. Support it with facts from history.

156

"A second-class intellect—but a first-class temperament."

Supreme Court Justice Oliver Wendell Holmes, Jr., used these words to describe Franklin Delano Roosevelt.

What does this quotation mean? Do you think that intelligence is the most important characteristic of an effective president? Can other personal characteristics sometimes be more important? Write one clear paragraph explaining your answer. Support it with examples from history.

157

"The worst thing about the camp was we felt we didn't have a country. We didn't know what we were, American or Japanese. We could have been very helpful in the defense work. Sitting in the camps like that didn't do us any good."

These words date from about 1942.
Who do you think might have said them? _____

Can a government ever justify locking up some of its citizens even if they have committed no crime? Explain your answer as fully as possible in one clear paragraph.

158

World War II was fought on several fronts, including North Africa and Italy. For each major military engagement below, write which country—and which section of that country—it occurred in.

1. Battles of Faid Pass and
    Kasserine Pass, February 1943 _____

2. Bizerte, May 1943 _____

3. Messina, August 1943 _____

4. Salerno, September 1943 _____

5. Naples, October 1943 _____

6. Anzio, January–May 1944 _____

159

In the summer of 1944, American and other Allied troops moved into France.

Ardennes forest	Omaha and Utah beaches
Caen	Saint-Lô
Cherbourg	

Match each military engagement below with the correct place name.

1. Under General Bradley, record numbers of U.S. and Allied troops land here in Normandy. They sustain heavy casualties but maintain a foothold. _____

2. Allies storm this town in Normandy in June, taking 35,000 German prisoners. _____

3. Allied forces beat back Rommel's men and take this Normandy city in July. The city is largely destroyed in the process. _____

4. Allies finally move beyond the Normandy beachheads into central France at this "gateway to the south." This allows troops to push toward Paris. _____

5. At the end of 1944, a final German offensive here is known as the Battle of the Bulge. _____

160

One of the major fronts of World War II was in the Pacific. Complete each statement by circling the letter of the correct answer.

1. At Pearl Harbor on December 7, 1941, (a) the Germans crippled the U.S. fleet. (b) the Japanese crippled the U.S. fleet. (c) President Roosevelt ordered the U.S. Navy to attack Japan.

2. In April and May of 1942, the Battle of Corregidor resulted in (a) American control of the Philippines. (b) American control of the Solomon Islands. (c) Japanese control of the Philippines.

3. At the Battle of Midway in June 1942, the American fleet kept Japan from taking Midway Island. This reduced the chances of another Japanese attack on (a) the East Coast of the U.S. (b) Hawaii. (c) Australia and New Zealand.

4. U.S. marines successfully resisted a Japanese attack here during the Battle of Guadalcanal in November 1942. This ended Japanese power in (a) the Solomon Islands. (b) Hawaii. (c) the Philippines.

5. In May 1943, U.S. troops won the Battle of Attu in the Aleutian Islands. They drove the Japanese out and ended further attempts at landing in (a) North America. (b) the Philippines. (c) the Solomon Islands.

161

© 2002 J. Weston Walch, Publisher

During the last two years of World War II, fierce fighting continued in the Pacific between American and Japanese forces. Match each military engagement on the left with the corresponding place name on the right.

1. February 1944: U.S. troops take these Pacific islands after heavy fighting. _____

2. June 1944: Admiral Ozawa of Japan turns back his fleet from their way to Saipan after losing almost all Japanese warplanes in this sea battle. _____

3. October 1944: In these Philippine coastal waters, the Japanese suffer their first major defeat after land battles go to the U.S. _____

4. February–March 1945: The Americans suffer heavy casualties, but their ultimate victory allows them to bomb Japan more aggressively from this southwest location. _____

5. April–June 1945: Japan fights U.S. forces from land and by air, in kamikaze attacks; the U.S. suffers thousands of casualties but manages to take this strategic island south of Japan. _____

(a) Okinawa

(b) Iwo Jima

(c) Marshall Islands

(d) Leyte Gulf

(e) Philippine Sea

During World War II, many women entered the workforce. They did this to help support their families and to keep war-related manufacturing efforts going. After the war, however, it was "back to the kitchen" for most of these women. Why? Give at least three reasons for this change.

163

Look at the graph below. It shows immigration to the United States between 1900 and 1950.

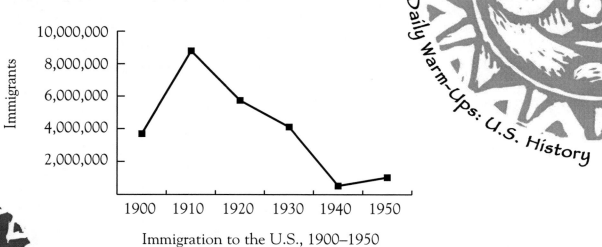

Immigration to the U.S., 1900–1950

164

What historical events or trends can you see reflected in the graph? Make at least two observations based on the data shown.

Millions of African Americans moved north after World War II. They were hoping for better jobs, better schools, better treatment from their white neighbors—better lives in general. During the 1950s, the black population of Chicago doubled. This made Chicago the city with the largest number of African Americans in the country. Like immigrants from overseas, these southern American immigrants usually moved into large urban areas.

What were some of the problems encountered by the African Americans who moved to northern cities? How did the cities themselves change as a result of this migration? While millions of black Americans were moving north into large cities, what were millions of white Americans doing? How did this affect many of the large northern cities during the 1960s? Write one clear paragraph explaining your answer. Provide examples to support your opinion.

165

© 2002 J. Weston Walch, Publisher

The Korean War was relatively brief, but brutal.

Communist powers invaded South Korea on June 24, 1950. President Truman called on the United Nations to help the United States defend the Korean peninsula. By the middle of August, there were 65,000 American ground troops in the area. They were supported by British and UN military forces. Ultimately, over 350,000 U.S. troops were involved in this so-called "police action."

For each location below, say whether it is in North Korea or South Korea.

Chipyong _____   Seoul _____

Chongchon River_____   Soyang _____

Osan _____   Yudam-ni _____

Pusan _____

". . . advertising has created an American frame of mind that makes people want more things, better things and newer things."

The president of the National Broadcasting Company made this statement in 1956. He was commenting on the increase in advertising since television became available after World War II.

Do you agree with the quotation? Is it more or less true today than it was in 1956? Explain your answer in one clear paragraph. Use examples from your own experience to back up your opinion.

167

After World War II, 12 million veterans returned home. This caused a "baby boom," which lasted through the early 1960s. During this period, the United States population grew by 30 percent (40 million people).

Any significant growth rate in a population is bound to have significant effects. In the case of the postwar baby boom, the effects were felt in many areas. They included the home, the workplace, public services, and the overall economic and social fabric of American society.

168

Think about how the baby boom affected children, younger adults, and older adults—and how it may still be affecting us today. List all the ways you think the baby boom affected these areas of American life. Include at least one effect in each area: home, work, public services, and society as a whole.

During the 1950s, suburbs in the United States grew six times faster than cities. By 1970, more Americans were living in suburbs than anywhere else.

The first large developer of suburban housing was a New Yorker named William Levitt. In 1947, he built thousands of mass-produced houses on Long Island, New York. However, Levittown (as it was called) excluded African Americans. Housing contracts ruled out "members of other than the Caucasian race."

Levittown was also primarily a place for young families. World War II veterans settled there with their new wives and babies. It did not attract many older people.

American suburbs have evolved since the early days of Levittown. However, they often still have some features of that early suburban model. Think of some of the suburbs in your community. How do they resemble the descriptions of Levittown above? How do they seem to be different? Do you think suburbs are basically a good thing? Explain your answer in one clear paragraph. Include examples to support your opinion.

169

© 2002 J. Weston Walch, Publisher

Study the following graph. Write your answers in one or two sentences below.

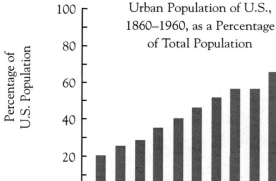

Urban Population of U.S., 1860–1960, as a Percentage of Total Population

Percentage of U.S. Population

100
80
60
40
20

1860 1880 1900 1920 1940 1960

170

The percentage for 1940 appears to be the same as for 1930. Every other decade shows an increase over the one before. What historic event or trend might this reflect?

There is an unusually large increase in percentage between 1940 and 1950. Why?

When does the percentage of people living in urban areas reach more than 50 percent? What historic trend might this reflect?

"The worst crime the white man has committed has been to teach us to hate ourselves."

These words were spoken by Malcolm X in the early 1960s.

Who was Malcolm X? What did the "X" stand for? How did Malcolm X help African Americans? Write one clear paragraph for your answer.

171

President Lyndon Johnson spoke of a "Great Society." In it, there would be no place for racism or poverty. During his administration, the United States Congress passed legislation to meet these goals. Some of those laws and programs are listed below.

Civil Rights Act of 1964

Housing and Urban
Development Act of 1965

Medicaid

Medicare

Voting Rights Act of 1965

172

In one or two sentences, explain the basic goal of each of these initiatives.

Which one do you think has had the greatest effect on the American people? Write one or two sentences explaining your answer.

The Vietnam War began for America with the Tonkin Gulf Resolution. Congress passed this in August 1964 after North Vietnamese ships attacked two U.S. destroyers. The war grew beyond all American expectations. As time passed, it met with strong public resistance. The last U.S. combat troops did not leave South Vietnam until August 1972. This was America's longest military engagement of the twentieth century.

Indicate whether each of the following statements is true or false.

___ 1. The Gulf of Tonkin is located between North Vietnam and China.

___ 2. The Ho Chi Minh Trail led from North Vietnam to Thailand.

___ 3. Heavy U.S. bombing of North Vietnam was relatively ineffective in fighting the Vietcong.

___ 4. The tide of war turned in favor of the U.S. when the Tet Offensive began on January 31, 1968.

___ 5. Negotiations for a cease-fire took place in Paris in May 1968. They did not result in the immediate end to fighting.

___ 6. President Lyndon Johnson authorized the beginning of the Vietnam War. President Richard Nixon authorized the ending.

173

Put the following events in the correct chronological order. Number the events from 1 to 7, with 1 the earliest event.

_____ (a) Robert F. Kennedy is assassinated.

_____ (b) First man on the moon

_____ (c) Watergate scandal

_____ (d) United States enters the Vietnam War

_____ (e) Cuban missile crisis

_____ (f) Martin Luther King, Jr. is assassinated

_____ (g) President John F. Kennedy is assassinated

174

The left column shows key dates in U.S. history related to voting rights. Match each date with the correct description in the right column.

1. 1789

2. 1820s–1830s

3. 1870 (Amendment 15)

4. 1920 (Amendment 19)

5. 1961 (Amendment 23)

6. 1971 (Amendment 26)

(a) People in the District of Columbia can vote in presidential elections.

(b) People over age 18 can vote.

(c) White men over 21 (with a certain amount of property) can vote.

(d) First in the western states, then in the eastern states, all white men are allowed to vote.

(e) Black men can vote.

(f) Women get the vote.

175

Put the following events in the correct chronological order. Number the events from 1 to 7, with 1 the earliest event.

____ (a) Iran-Contra affair

____ (b) fall of the Berlin Wall

____ (c) Three Mile Island nuclear accident

____ (d) Iranian hostage crisis

    ____ (e) first terrorist attack (bombing) at World Trade Center

    ____ (f) Persian Gulf crisis

    ____ (g) second terrorist attack (by plane) at World Trade Center

176

Many countries include different ethnic groups. Conflicts between these groups can create internal difficulties. These disputes can even break a nation apart. This happened in Yugoslavia, which fell apart in 1991.

Name two other places where ethnic conflicts threaten the country's stability. What political advice would you give the leader of one of these countries? Can a government's constitution allow for differences to be aired, while still maintaining the peace and guaranteeing equal rights for all groups? Can parts of the United States Constitution serve as a guide? Write a clear paragraph to explain your answer. Use examples to support your opinion.

177

© 2002 J. Weston Walch, Publisher

The Arab oil embargo of 1973 affected the United States. Suddenly drivers faced long lines at the gas pump and high gas prices.

Why was the embargo called for? Who called for it? What should the United States do to avoid another oil crisis in the future? Write your answer in one clear paragraph.

178

Three times in American history, the Senate has either considered or has carried out impeachment proceedings against the president.

What is *impeachment*? Check the definition in a history book with a glossary or in a dictionary. Then write the definition in your own words.

Which three presidents were either considered for impeachment or were impeached? What was the outcome in each case? Write one or two sentences about each one.

179

On September 11, 2001, the worst attack on the United States in history took place. The horrific assault was a well-coordinated effort. It took place at almost the same time in three different parts of the country. Thousands of people were killed within hours. Thousands more were injured.

How were the attacks conducted? What was the significance of the targets? Write one clear paragraph explaining your answer.

President George W. Bush said of this attack, "This is a different kind of war." What did he mean? Write one clear paragraph explaining your answer.

180

Answers will vary on pages not listed.

1. 1. dendrochronology; 2. carbon-14 dating
2. 1. T; 2. F (They would have used the Bering Strait, not the Baltic Strait.); 3. F (They lived mostly in caves.); 4. T; 5. T; 6. F (They did not engage in trade.)
3. Maya: Mexico, Guatemala, El Salvador, Honduras; Aztec: Mexico; Inca: Peru; Chibcha: Colombia; Toltec: Mexico
4. 1. cashew; 2. hurricane; 3. barbecue; 4. hammock
5. bow and arrow, pottery, game like Hindu *parchesi*, boats made from reeds
6. 3 (a); 1 (b); 5 (c); 6 (d); 4 (e); 7 (f); 2 (g)
7. maize, tobacco, chocolate, peanuts, cassava, kidney and lima beans.
8. 1. chocolate; 2. tomato; 3. coyote; 4. chile (or chili)
9. There was a surface resemblance to Egyptian architecture—for example, in the stepped pyramid style of the temples in Central and South America. In addition, there was a certain European arrogance about native peoples of the New World and their lack of ability to create anything as sophisticated as the structures the early explorers saw.
10. These mounds had multiple purposes but were most often used for garbage dumps, foundations for buildings, and as burial sites. After about 700 C.E., the mounds were often shaped like birds, snakes, and other creatures. From the remains of the dead found inside some mounds, it is clear that these tribal peoples had elaborate death-related rituals. (As a point of interest, the Cahokia mound in East Saint Louis, Missouri, is 100 feet high and covers 16 acres.)
11. Fish played a critical role in the economy and health of the northwest coastal tribes. The innovation was smoking, a technique that enabled them to preserve the fish for many

Daily Warm-Ups: U.S. History

weeks. This allowed these Native Americans to control their food supply and to store up enough food to last them through the winter and other times of scarcity. This resulted in the creation of a certain amount of leisure time.

12. <u>2</u> (a); <u>3</u> (b); <u>1</u> (c)

13. 1. caribou; 2. hominy; 3. hickory; 4. chipmunk

14. The original five nations were the Mohawk, Cayuga, Oneida, Onondaga, and Seneca. The sixth was the Tuscarora tribe.

15. There is a striking similarity to the preamble to the U.S. Constitution. Other answers will vary, but there are many examples in history of ideas—and even specific language—carrying over from one group or individual to another. The Declaration of Independence also has such "carryovers."

16. Answers include: A. Northeast—Abenaki, Cayuga, Delaware, Erie, Huron, Massachusetts, Mohawk, Seneca, Susquehanna, Tuscarora; B. Southeast—Algonquian, Apalachee, Caddo, Calusa, Catawba, Cherokee, Chickasaw, Choctaw, Creek, Guale, Muskogee, Natchez, Quapaw, Seminole; C. Northwest—Cayuse, Chumash, Nez Perce, Nootka, Paiute, Shoshone; D. Southwest—Atakapa, Apache, Chiricahua, Comanche, Mohave, Papagao, Pima, Wichita, Zuni; E. Plains and Central—Arapaho, Cheyenne, Chippewa, Crow, Dakota, Fox, Illinois, Iowa, Kansa, Kickapoo, Kiowa, Miami, Missouri, Osage, Ottawa, Pawnee, Potawatomi, Santee, Sauk, Shawnee, Teton, Ute, Winnebago, Wyandot

18. Magellan proved that the earth was round. He was also the first to sail around the world and the first to find Asia by sailing west. He gave Spain an advantage in terms of new land

to acquire. Da Gama, on the other hand, found the shortest and best sea route to Asia. He was the first to find Asia by sea. Although he did not give Portugal the advantage in terms of new land, he gave them the advantage in terms of wealth (through trade).

19. (a) 1497; (b) 1493; (c) 1497; (d) 1502; (e) c. 1000; (f) 1492; (g) 1513

20. England was at war with Spain from 1587 to 1604, so her resources were tied up with events in Europe.

21. The caravel is a ship with a pointed bow. It could sail very close to the wind—a necessary feature for anyone trying to cross the Atlantic, which required continuous tacking. Caravels were rigged with lateen sails, which were triangular in shape. The caravel didn't require such a large crew for rowing because it could move almost as quickly as a modern racing sailboat. Thus the caravel went farther and faster with fewer people.

22. Columbus was certain that he would find a shorter route to Asia by sailing west. He thought that the Asians would not speak Latin (the European common language in the fifteenth century), but hoped that they might speak Arabic, due to their relative proximity to Arab regions and their trade connections.

23. Columbus set up a forced labor system with his fellow Europeans (mostly Spaniards who had voyaged with him). He divided up the land (with the Native Americans on it) among the colonists. They in turn demanded regular tributes of gold, which the natives were unable to produce in adequate quantities. The colonists killed thousands of natives outright, allowed thousands of others to die of disease and abuse, and shipped many others off as slaves. Thus there arose the need to import slaves to the Caribbean region in

order to work the sugar and cotton plantations and to prospect for gold.

24. The resource was codfish. The area of the
Grand Banks was especially productive, but
this species was plentiful all along the northeast coast of North America. The cod has
fairly sturdy flesh, which made it especially
good for smoking and curing and shipping
back to Europe. Fishermen learned how to
cure the fish on shore just after it was caught.

25. De Soto's body went to the bottom of the
Mississippi River, never to be seen again. His
soldiers did this because they could not let
the Native Americans see the physical proof
of his death. The Spaniards—like most other
Europeans—showed arrogance toward the
native peoples, taking their land and food as
needed, but giving little in return. They had
no scruples about lying to the Indians and
felt that the myth about de Soto's godlike

qualities would allow them to take better
advantage.

26. North America did not provide the gold and
silver that Spain had hoped for. Moreover,
there was a great deal of unrest in Mexico
with the native populations; managing this
took up a great deal of Spain's resources.
Ultimately, Spain chose to exploit the large
populations in Mexico and Peru rather than
native peoples farther north. Most Spanish
colonists in North America were either
religious or military in nature (establishing
church missions and forts), and they were
overwhelmingly male. Spain did not encour-
age manufacturing in the New World, being
more interested in religious conversion.

27. Roanoke was not an ideal choice for a settlement. It had a relatively poor climate (being
swampy, humid, and insect-infested), and it
offered little real protection from the sur-

rounding Indians. The Native American population in that vicinity was large, and the natives were resentful of the numerous English demands for food and labor. Moreover, the second group of colonists were virtually ignored for three years by their mother country while Britain's ships were occupied in Europe fighting Spain.

28. For the most part, the French did not establish permanent settlements in North America—other than Quebec, Montreal, St. Louis, and New Orleans, which were all situated in key locations along the two most important riverways in the eastern half of the continent. The French were more interested in fur trapping and trading posts than in real colonies. By 1750, the population of the English colonies totaled 1.5 million; the French population was 80,000.

29. 1. John Smith; 2. William Bradford; 3. John Winthrop; 4. Lord Baltimore; 5. John Hooker; 6. Roger Williams

30. Reasons should include at least some of the following: England's cities were becoming crowded, with many poor and unemployed; Britain needed gold and other precious metals; Britain hoped that the colonies could provide natural resources and trading products that were being imported from Europe and Asia at great expense; Britain was looking for new markets for its wool products (which settlers and Indians could use); Britain wanted to spread Protestantism instead of the Catholicism being spread by the French and Spanish.

31. Answers will vary. However, this shipment of women was a huge success.

32. They bought 20 African slaves—the first black slaves in the North American colonies.

33. They paid their debts by making handsome

profits through fur trading. The sites were chosen at least in part because of their proximity to both rich trapping areas and good waterways.

34. 1. colonists from Massachusetts; seeking religious freedom, trading, and fishing; 2. the Netherlands and Sweden; looking for economic opportunity and land; 3. and 4. England; friends of the royal Stuart family, given land grants and looking for economic opportunity; 5. England; looking for economic opportunity and land; 6. England—mostly Quakers; looking for religious freedom and safety; 7. England; many were bankrupt looking for new economic opportunities

35. The French were mostly male and were generally explorers or trappers. They often adopted Indian dress, speech, and customs, and even married into Native American tribes on occasion. The French had more genuine respect for Indian ways. In addition, they were not usually interested in acquiring native land for colonizing; they used the land in a more nomadic way. The French also acted as diplomats in some Indian intertribal quarrels. The English, on the other hand, were colonists, including men, women, and children. They tended to be fearful of Native Americans and regarded them generally as inferior beings. The English wanted Indian land and resources in order for their colonies to survive; this led to conflict.

36. 1. (d); 2. (b); 3. (c); 4. (a)

37. 1. Southern colonies; 2. Middle colonies; 3. New England colonies

38. 1. (B); 2. (C); 3. (B); 4. (A); 5. (A); 6. (C); 7. (B); 8. (A)

39. The New England colonies and the Southern colonies were involved in triangular trade. New England system: Traders bought

molasses, grain, etc., in the Caribbean and shipped these products to New England. They sold them there for rum and ship products, which in turn they took to Africa. In Africa, the rum and ship products were sold for slaves. The slaves were shipped to the Caribbean, where they were sold for molasses, grain, etc. <u>Southern system</u>: Traders bought agricultural products (tobacco, rice, cotton) in the South and shipped them to England. There they were sold for manufactured goods (fabrics, iron products), which were shipped to Africa. In Africa, these goods were sold for slaves, who were shipped to the Southern colonies.

40. 1. imports; 2. apprentice; 3. colony; 4. manufacturing
41. 1. exports; 2. tariff; 3. textiles; 4. indentured servant
42. Massachusetts Bay Colony included a number of busy towns, including Boston, which were centers of society, commerce, and political thought. Virginia was largely rural—as was the entire South, which was based on a farming economy. In addition, Boston (unlike the South) was a center of learning even in the seventeenth century, with many schools and a university. These factors all led to more "news," and a corresponding interest in communication, in the Boston area.
43. 1. (c); 2. (a); 3. (b); 4. (a)
44. 1. bowling; 2. horse racing; 3. lacrosse; 4. fencing; 5. foxhunting; 6. horseshoes
45. 1. (e); 2. (a); 3. (g); 4. (c); 5. (b); 6. (d); 7. (f)
46. Answers should include all or most of the following rivers: Wisconsin, Iowa, Illinois, Ohio, Cumberland, Tennessee, Arkansas, Red.
47. Mississippi, Missouri, Connecticut
49. Acadia was the region in the Canadian Maritimes now known as Nova Scotia. After

the Treaty of Paris, the Acadians were brutally expelled from their home by the English government. Some settled in English colonies nearby, some returned to France, and some migrated to French Louisiana (in the New Orleans area), where their name ("Acadians") became slurred over time into "Cajuns."

50. (a) 1763; (b) 1759; (c) 1755; (d) 1754; (e) 1756; (f) 1758

51. The Treaty of Paris was so sweeping in its victorious claims of land for Britain, and so punitive in its treatment of France, that it caused France to give up virtually all power in colonial America. However, the French were so disturbed by the outcome of the conflict that it left them disposed to ally themselves with the colonists against the British a little more than a decade later, when the Revolutionary War began.

52. 1. (b); 2. (a); 3. (d); 4. (c)

53. 1. (d); 2. (a); 3. (b); 4. (c)

54. 1. (d); 2. (b); 3. (a); 4. (c)

55. Paine was referring to the challenges of being ruled by an overseas government. In the eighteenth century, transportation and communication technologies were limited to slow ships and handwritten letters. This meant long periods of waiting for an answer from Britain before the colonists could act—even when the situation was urgent.

56. 1. treason; 2. boycott; 3. allies; 4. repeal

57. 1. revenue-generating laws; 2. negotiations; 3. trade laws; 4. radicals

58. Answers will vary, but humor has traditionally been considered an effective political tool.

59. 1. (d); 2. (c); 3. (a); 4. (e); 5. (b)

60. Franklin was referring to "Mother" England and the Colonists' growing frustration that she was preventing them from "growing up," or becoming independent.

61. British losses were nearly 48 percent; Colonial losses were 14 percent. The British learned that the colonists were passionate about their cause—and better skilled on the battlefield than anticipated. After this fight, British troops loosened up their rigid formations and adapted their battle tactics somewhat in order to avoid a repeat of the slaughter.

62. Some reasons for the loss include: the British were brightly dressed and easy for their opponents to spot; the weather was very hot, causing physical discomfort to the uniformed British men and slowing them down; the colonists were at an advantage, since they were at the top of the hill; the British soldiers marched in tight formation, offering virtual "walls" of color at which to shoot; the colonists maintained the discipline to wait until they could see "the whites of their eyes," before firing, which worked well. In fact, if the Americans had not run out of gunpowder, it is likely that they would have driven the British off altogether.

63. 1A: E; 1B: C; 2A: C; 2B: E; 3A: E; 3B: C

64. The speaker was John Adams. He was trying to persuade Jefferson to write the draft of the Declaration of Independence. Adams believed that Jefferson was the best choice because he himself (Adams) was known for his caustic comments and ability to offend people. Jefferson was more diplomatic; he was also known as a talented writer. Furthermore, Adams thought that it was important to have a Virginian heavily involved in writing the Declaration to win over the votes of the southern delegates.

65. Advantages: larger army; larger navy; more money; better trained soldiers; more political influence. Disadvantages: not all British troops went to the colonies; not all British

ships went to the colonies; England was thousands of miles away; transporting soldiers, etc., took months; British troops needed to stay near water if they wanted to get supplies; colonists were fighting on their home turf and knew it better; colonists fought in some non-traditional ways that worked well in northeastern terrain.

66. Stark is urging his troops to fight harder and more bravely than the paid mercenaries (Hessians) on the British side. He is belittling their value as soldiers by mentioning the price they were paid for their service. Stark challenges his men to prove their true "worth," not in dollar value, but in fighting with great courage. He claims that either the colonists will win the battle and take the hill in question, or he at least will die in the attempt.

67. Colonial soldiers were volunteers who were essentially able to leave active service when-

ever they needed to. This could be a great inconvenience to their officers and to the overall management of the army. Their numbers increased and decreased with the seasons because many Continental Army members were farmers. They returned home in the spring and fall for sowing and harvest.

68. The other half consisted of Hessians and Native Americans. Burgoyne lost the battle because his troops were attacked aggressively on the way to Saratoga by colonial soldiers hiding in the heavily wooded areas of rural New York. Their route was also blocked by deliberately felled trees. Burgoyne used too many supplies just in getting his men to Saratoga. Moreover, the planned rendezvous with General Howe and his troops did not happen.

69. Key effects included the following: the French brought the Continental Army better leader-

ship (through the French generals and other officers), better weapons, a bigger army and navy (augmented now by the French troops), and more money and supplies.

70. 1. Lexington and Concord (spring 1775—first battle of the war); 2. Valley Forge (winter 1777–78—low point for Continental Army, but they survived and got stronger, more unified as an army); 3. Saratoga (autumn 1777—convinced the French to form alliance with the colonists); 4. Yorktown (autumn 1781—exactly four years after the Battle of Saratoga—last major battle of the war; persuaded British to stop fighting)

71. 1. Cornwallis; 2. Howe; 3. Burgoyne; 4. Gage; 5. Carleton

72. 1. France; 2. Prussia; 3. Prussia; 4. France; 5. Poland; 6. Poland

73. Many wealthy people had made personal loans to the fledgling government and had not been paid back. They were especially interested in seeing a stronger federal government with the ability to establish and collect taxes, enforce laws, and ensure that all states followed the same laws.

74. fight wars, form armies, print and borrow money, make decisions about Native Americans, establish a postal service; Answers to the second part of the warm-up will vary.

75. 1. legislature; 2. ratify; 3. constitution; 4. simple majority; 5. plurality; 6. confederation

76. The six goals: to form a more perfect union; establish justice; ensure domestic tranquility; provide for the common defense; promote the general welfare; secure liberty. Other answers will vary.

77. 1. amendment; 2. precedent; 3. federal; 4. appropriate

78. 1. constituents; 2. standing committee; 3. joint committee; 4. legislation;

5. commerce

79. The South, with its huge slave population, wanted slaves to count as full members of the population so that southern states would be allotted more votes in Congress. The North did not want slaves to count at all. The South did not want slaves to count as property, since that would require taxation; the North wanted slaves to be counted as property and wanted southern slaveowners to pay taxes accordingly. The southern states showed hypocrisy by claiming that slaves should not be counted as property, when in fact slaves were just that—the property of the slave-owners, with virtually none of the benefits of citizenship.

80. North: No, No, Yes, No; South: Yes, Yes, No, Yes; North and South were diametrically opposed in each category. These differences would help lead to the Civil War.

81. Compromise 1: the Great Compromise—the houses of Congress will be divided, with states getting two senators each and a variable number of members of congress (depending on state population). Compromise 2: Slaves will be counted as 3/5 of a person each. Compromise 3: Federal government gets control over trade, but agrees not to make laws about the slave trade until 1808. It also will not tax exports or interstate trade products.

82. 1. compromise; 2. bill; 3. veto; 4. legislative; 5. executive; 6. judicial; 7. override; 8. impeach

83. First amendment. Other answers will vary.

84. 1. lawyer; someone qualified to act in legal proceedings on behalf of someone else; 2. money given the court to guarantee that an accused person will return for trial; 3. one person sues another; 4. state or federal government tries someone who is accused of a

crime; 5. being tried twice for the same offense

85. 1. someone against whom a legal action is taken and who must explain his or her side; 2. group of citizens who hear evidence and decide whether there is enough to warrant a trial; 3. a good, compelling reason; 4. document that allows police to search someone's property; 5. document that legally requires someone to appear in court

87. <u>Stamp Act</u>: protests were made to Britain (then ruler of the colonies); all 13 colonies supported the protests; protests were largely peaceful, although harassment of tax collectors did happen; methods used were boycotting and assembling a congress (in New York) to ask for repeal. Outcome: act was repealed. <u>Whiskey Tax</u>: protests were made to new American government; only small farmers in certain regions (like western Pennsylvania) were involved; some protests became violent (tarring and feathering, destruction of machinery of farmers who paid the tax); methods used were refusing to pay, marching into court, marching in Pittsburgh. Outcome: militia was sent in by George Washington to stop rebellion, and tax continued.

88. Johnny is John Adams. Georgy is George Washington. Adams is currently president, and Thomas Jefferson will be competing against him in the coming election. These Jefferson supporters imply that Adams is not democratic enough, perhaps with leanings toward monarchy.

89. 1. foreign (or foreigner); 2. a tie (as seen in jury votes or elections); 3. the Supreme Court reviews laws passed by Congress to make sure they are constitutional; 4. to let alone; for the government not to be very involved; 5. stir-

ring people up against the government; 6. not allowed by the Constitution

90. Lafayette was paying homage to Washington as the father of the new American democracy and as a military leader who had been instrumental in winning the war for independence. He was also acknowledging the effect that American democratic thought had had on France during the French Revolution in 1789. A memorable event of the French Revolution was the destruction of the Bastille by the citizens of Paris. By giving the key to Washington, Lafayette was implying that Washington helped lead the French people to freedom by his example.

91. Isolationism. Other answers will vary, but with the increasing interconnectedness of the modern world, it is unlikely that isolationism would be an effective policy for any nation.

92. He left out his term as president of the United States, and his role in arranging the Louisiana Purchase. Perhaps he was most proud of his work in writing the Declaration and in founding the University of Virginia, as education was something about which Jefferson cared passionately.

93. Answers should include references to buildings that are symmetrical, columned and/or pedimented, possibly domed, and constructed with limestone or marble. National landmarks exhibiting this style include the U.S. Capitol building, the Supreme Court building, the Lincoln and Jefferson memorials, and Monticello.

95. The Virginia Planter presidents were Washington, Jefferson, Madison, and Monroe. All were from the state of Virginia, and all were landowners and wealthy farmers.

96. The Prophet and his followers were massacred by U.S. army soldiers. Essentially, there was

no effective way for Native Americans to recapture their traditional way of life at this point in history. White encroachment and government seizure of their property were increasingly inevitable. The U.S. government regarded both the Prophet and and his brother Tecumseh as threats to the peaceful settlement of the West and wanted these threats eliminated.

97. Tecumseh played an important role in the War of 1812 as an advisor and scout for the British. All other answers will vary.

98. The British blockade forced the United States to develop new industries, and to strengthen existing ones, because Americans could not import the foreign goods they needed. Examples of the kinds of industry that began to flourish in America are textiles and gun manufacturing.

99. 1. E; 2. C; 3. C; 4. E; 5. E; 6. C; 7. C

100. The song commemorates a battle of the War of 1812 in which Oliver Hazard Perry and his men won control of Lake Erie from the British. Winning control of Lake Erie gave the Americans critical water access to the Great Lakes, the St. Lawrence River, and therefore Canada.

101. As a general during the War of 1812, Jackson led the outnumbered American troops with great spirit to defeat the British at the Battle of New Orleans on January 8, 1815. This was the last major campaign of the British in the war. Other nicknames include Old Hickory, Sharp Knife, and Pointed Arrow.

103. *Slavery* here means the southern states having to bow to the will of Congress and the U.S. government and to pay taxes against their will. The speaker certainly seems to be urging that the South defy the tax; he is also probably advocating secession. South Carolina

did nullify the 1828 and 1832 Tariff Acts, although this was overruled by President Jackson. South Carolina was also the first state actually to secede from the Union (in 1860); it was known for a long time as "the cradle of secession."

104. The hydra was a many-headed monster in Greek mythology. When the hero Hercules cut off one of the hydra's heads, two new heads grew back in its place. This is an appropriate metaphor for the bank, which had numerous branches and seemed to be multiplying at an alarming rate.

105. Yes, the Associated Press still exists. Advantages include: efficient; economical; does the news-gathering for small papers that can't afford their own national or international reporters; covers territory that most papers would otherwise not cover. Disadvantages include: potential for slanted news (only one source giving you the information); lack of competition can lead to complacency and sloppy reporting; no variety in the news reporting from one paper (or one city) to another for all topics covered by this service.

106. 1. (h); 2. (g); 3. (c); 4. (e); 5. (b); 6. (a); 7. (d); 8. (f)

107. 1. mule driver who would lead mules towing barges and boats through canals; 2. well-equipped passenger steamboat; 3. young woman who worked in the mills in Lowell, Massachusetts; 4. road made of logs set in parallel fashion over swampy or muddy area; 5. machine that allowed textile workers to spin several threads at once

108. This poem paints far too rosy a picture of life in the mills. Although there were some "model" factory communities (Lowell was designed to be one), most were not.

110. Answers will vary. However, since the advent

of television in the twentieth century, accusations that the media helps to trivialize political campaigns have run rampant. One such example can be taken from the campaign for the breathtakingly close 2000 presidential election. During the campaign, George W. Bush was portrayed as a simple Texas "boy" who shunned the East Coast (with its elitist institutions) and avoided big-city life—particularly in Washington, with its political intrigues and "insider" qualities. In reality, of course, although Bush did spend much of his life in Texas, he was descended from two upper-class East Coast families, was educated at elite East Coast schools, and spent every summer at a family estate in Maine. Moreover, he was no stranger to Washington, having been very much involved with both the campaign and the administration of his father.

111. This song was written during the presidential campaign of 1844. It was written for the new (and very small) Liberty party, which was promoting the strongly antislavery candidate, James G. Birney. The song suggests that opponent Henry Clay would not take a firm stand on the annexation of Texas (Clay was known as the Great Compromiser). It also reminds people that James Polk supported the slave system in the South and wanted to annex Texas (which the Liberty party opposed).

112. A paraphrase might read: "Human history is a long series of stories in which men have abused the rights of women." The similarity in wording between the Declaration of Sentiments and the Declaration of Independence was probably meant to cloak the ideas of this convention in time-honored, highly respectable—and patriotic—language, and also perhaps to mock the chauvinistic attitudes of the founding fathers. Other

answers will vary.

113. The largest group of immigrants was Irish. Ireland had suffered from economic depression for most of the early 1900s. This condition worsened greatly, reaching catastrophic proportions, when the Irish potato crop suffered from potato blight in 1845.

114. Answers include the following: America wanted Cuba's sugar plantations; America wanted to expand its territories; it was empire-building, extending into the Caribbean area; the South was especially interested in Cuba because Cuba also allowed slavery (for its plantation economy), and this might be a way for the South to expand its holdings to counterbalance the abolitionist North.

115. Answers will vary, but may include: *Oliver Twist* by Charles Dickens; the *Diary of a Young Girl* by Anne Frank; *Silent Spring* by Rachel Carson.

116. Lincoln was clearly referring to slavery, which he considered unjust and untenable. His position, which became the official Union position once he was elected president, was in direct opposition to that of his southern political rivals. Again, history is full of examples of political oppression by one group over another.

117. His prediction came true in part: It took the Union longer to win the war than Scott had thought, but the Union did succeed in encircling the Confederacy with naval blockades (using the Mississippi River, the Gulf of Mexico, and the Atlantic Ocean). This prevented troops and supplies from moving either in or out. In addition, the progression of Civil War battles moved in a basically circular direction, again reflecting the anaconda analogy.

119. Boston had roots going back to the first colonizing of America. The Boston area was the birthplace of the American Revolution; thus it could be considered a cradle of democracy, as was ancient Athens. Moreover, Boston was considered the literary and educational capital of the country (as was ancient Athens); many fine writers and many of the country's best schools were to be found there. Like Athens, Boston had also produced many fine statesmen who were early leaders of the country (for example, John Adams and John Hancock).

120. The Know-Nothings had evolved from a secret patriotic society that began in 1849. When people asked members about their secret club, their response was always that they didn't know anything about it—hence the name Know-Nothing. Nativism is an extreme political philosophy that favors native-born citizens over immigrants. Patriotism is the demonstration of love and staunch support for one's country. While patriotism can also become extreme under certain circumstances, it does not have the exclusive, potentially racist connotations that nativism does.

121. *Sullied* means dirtied or defiled. *Ermine* refers to the white fur that trimmed the ceremonial robes of judges, royalty, and so on (in this case, the reference is to judges). The critics were implying that the Southern judges had tarnished the honor of the court by giving in to their biases and proslavery political inclinations. Other examples might include the role that both the Florida Supreme Court and the U.S. Supreme Court played in the presidential election of 2000.

122. He was referring to the "house" (the United States) being divided between North and

South, and the impossibility of the nation remaining stable or secure should the two sides part ways. Using the metaphor of a house helped Lincoln remind people that they were all one family living together under one "roof" (the United States of America and its Constitution). He used ordinary language that all people could understand and identify with.

123. *Civilized* here refers to American Indians who had allowed themselves to be displaced and put on reservations. Other answers will vary, but it is unlikely that American Indians today would agree that this use of the word was appropriate.

124. George Washington, along with his wife, Martha, were to have been buried there. However, they were buried at Mount Vernon and remain there today. The crypt holds sculpture and exhibits instead.

125. In 1859, before the start of the Civil War, there were 33 states in the Union. "Bleeding" Kansas joined in 1861. By 1862, 11 states had seceded, leaving the total number of states in the Union at 23. Winthrop is urging that the nation be reunited as one and that the seceded states rejoin the Union.

126. 1861: First Battle of Bull Run; 1862: Battle of Shiloh, Second Battle of Bull Run, Battle of Antietam, Battle of Fredericksburg; 1863: Siege of Vicksburg, Gettysburg Address, Battle of Chattanooga, Emancipation Proclamation; 1864: Battle of Fort Morgan; 1865: Battle of Five Forks

127. He fears being found near the living quarters after daybreak, not working quickly enough in the fields, not picking enough cotton and having it weighed at the gin house, and oversleeping in the morning. All of these "faults" were brutally punished by whipping and other

means. Other answers will vary.

128. The Civil War occurred. During the war, the South abandoned its cash crop production (tobacco, sugar, and cotton) in order to grow enough food to supply its people and its military forces. The plantation system was also destroyed by the war: the land was destroyed, and slavery was made illegal. Finally, the southern transportation system—especially its rail lines—was ruined.

129. The original settlers often sold their claims very quickly to railroad corporations, speculators, and large-scale cattle ranchers. Some reasons include the following: the land was cheap, but farm supplies were very expensive, as were horses and wagons. Moreover, there were harsh natural elements facing these settlers: lack of water, prairie fires, pests—especially locusts, tornadoes, etc. Much of the land turned out to be good only for cattle raising, so farming ended up being more of a subsistence situation.

130. The key event was the Civil War. During (and just after) the war, the North and West experienced tremendous growth in the amount of railroad track laid. The industrial North and the resource-rich West were connected by rail to promote the easy flow of manufactured goods and food products and to facilitate settlement of western lands. The South was left largely out of this network. However, between 1880 and 1890, 25,000 more miles of track were laid in the South in an effort to expand their transportation network.

131. 1. (c); 2. (b); 3. (a)

132. 1. (a); 2. (d); 3. (b); 4. (e); 5. (c)

133. Answers should include some of the following: the North gave less political support to the South, especially southern African

Americans; there was large-scale unemployment in the North, which occupied most of the northern interests. Also, because of the depression, northern voters were unhappy with the Republicans—who had passed the Reconstruction legislation—and voted most of them out. As a result Southern whites, who were generally Democrats, now had their supporters in office. The government also had less money to spend on African-American programs during the depression. All in all, these changes left southern blacks more subject to abuse, loss of office, and obstruction of voting rights and economic opportunities.

134. 1. Navajo; 2. Apache; 3. Cheyenne
135. Answers should include references to the increasing pressure being applied by the U.S. government to American Indian tribes in an effort to wrest native lands away from the Indians. With the discovery of silver, gold,

and other valuable natural resources, and with the government's desire to expand and settle the nation (and eliminate the risk of Indian attacks), the U.S. government was ruthless in its efforts to relocate American Indians. These conflicts represent the Indians' last-ditch efforts to save their land and their way of life.

136. Mexican Americans: Yes (by treaty); No (generally); Yes (railroad work, mining, ranching, other industries); Yes (became automatic citizens, intermarried with whites, moved to urban areas in large numbers). Native Americans: No (moved to reservations); Yes (fairly frequently); No (given small, insufficient annuities, became dependent); No (nearly complete segregation)

137. 1. the East Coast and the Great Lakes; 2. the Appalachian Mountains; 3. East Coast: international seaports, consumer good industries,

financial centers; Great Lakes: steel and steel products, railroad centers, oil refining

139. They are the poor of society, who were generally ignored by the movers and shakers of the world. Yes, journalists today can—and often do—serve the same function. Other answers will vary.

141. Answers will vary, but Rockefeller clearly exhibits extreme arrogance and a feeling of moral superiority over poorer Americans. He insensitively equates wealth with virtue rather than opportunity and education.

142. 1. (b); 2. (c); 3. (a)

143. All these corporations were monopolies formed during the late 1800s. They squeezed out small business owners, but strengthened the production power and efficiency of the country's industries. The specialty of three of the companies is obvious from their names: oil, tobacco, and telephones. The other two

are: Northern Securities Corporation, which controlled the railroads, and the Armour Company, which controlled meat packing.

144. 1. (d); 2. (e); 3. (a); 4. (b); 5. (f); 6. (c)

146. Both depressions were caused by an oversupply of goods and too much expansion. The effect was an increase in the number of monopolies in the country.

147. Answers will vary, but socioeconomic conditions are not healthy as described by Weaver. The two classes he mentions are the tramps (with whom the Populists identified) and the millionaires—an exaggeration, certainly, but with a valid point.

148. France and Great Britain both had bigger navies. Roosevelt realized the massive power of the growing American industrial base and was determined to make the United States a major trading partner in the world economy. He wanted more naval bases

and more territory from which to "defend national interests."

149. 1. (b); 2. (c); 3. (a)

150. 1. imperialism; 2. nationalism; 3. diplomacy; 4. domination; 5. accommodation

151. 1. New York and Philadelphia appear in both graphs. However, Philadelphia has slipped from second place in 1820 to third place in 1900. 2. Baltimore is listed third in 1820, but its place has been taken by Chicago by 1900. Answers will vary, but they should include some reference to the westward migration of the American population during the nineteenth century, replacing older colonial cities in the east like Baltimore with newer, midwestern urban areas like Chicago. 3. Other observations might include the phenomenal growth of New York City, a reflection of the huge waves of immigration to hit that East Coast destination during the nineteenth

century.

152. At the time of World War I, the largest recent immigrant groups in the United States were Germans and Italians. They naturally felt torn between loyalty to their new country, America, and their countries of origin—Germany and Italy—which were two of the Central Powers. More "rooted" Americans who had been in the country for several generations or longer, many of whom were of English, Irish, Scottish, or Scandinavian stock, were generally predisposed to favor the Allies.

153. German Foreign Secretary Zimmermann wrote the telegram to the German foreign minister in Mexico. The text basically promised financial and political aid to Mexico if it would invade the United States and try to reacquire Texas, New Mexico, and Arizona. Germany's motive here was to create a large

diversion in North America so that the United States would be less likely to join forces with the Allies in Europe.

154. 1. (c) (July 18–August 6); 2. (b) (August 19–November 11); 3. (a) (September 12–16); 4. (d) (September 20–November 11); 5. (e) (October 24–November 1)

155. 1. The heavy buying and use of credit depleted people's personal savings. When the depression hit, they were unable to pay their regular bills and could not make the interest payments on their loans. 2. This consolidation meant that when one corporation failed, it failed on a massive scale, causing large numbers of unemployed people at one time. The bankruptcy of a single corporation affected thousands. Moreover, because of the trend toward monopolies in most industrial sectors, there were very few competing companies able to step into the breach when a corpora-tion failed. 3. When the richest and biggest-spending sector of the population lost much of its money, it had none left to pump into the weak economy, further accelerating the downturn.

156. These names were used with dark humor because people tended to blame President Hoover for the Great Depression. Since many of the poorest citizens ended up on the streets or in shantytowns, they had few (if any) of the necessities of life, including blankets to ward off the cold night air. They resorted to using newspapers—hence the name "Hoover blankets." In fact, Hoover had little to do with the economic factors creating the Depression. He had only been inaugurated president in 1929, and after his election he tried (with limited success) to spur job growth, force financial institutions to give easier credit terms, and reduce taxes as quick-

ly as possible.

157. This quotation, while somewhat stinging, makes an interesting statement about the qualities that are most essential in a leader, particularly during times of crisis. Roosevelt was certainly not unintelligent; on the other hand, he was not known as an academic. Holmes implies that Roosevelt's intellect was sufficient for the job, but that what was much more important was his warm, reassuring personality—his ability to instill trust and hope in the American people. This was something that had been lacking in the Hoover administration, and it was a critical psychological factor in helping Americans work their way out of the Depression and gear up for World War II.

158. Answers will vary, but the words were spoken by a Japanese American who was placed in an internment camp in the western United States during World War II.

159. 1. Tunisia; 2. Tunisia; 3. Sicily (Italy); 4. Italy (southwest coast); 5. Italy (southwest coast, just above Salerno); 6. Italy (west coast, just south of Rome)

160. 1. Omaha and Utah beaches; 2. Cherbourg; 3. Caen; 4. Saint-Lô; 5. Ardennes forest

161. 1. (b); 2. (c); 3. (b); 4. (a); 5. (a)

162. 1. (c); 2. (e); 3. (d); 4. (b); 5. (a)

163. Answers should include at least some of the following: returning veterans needed their old jobs back; the return of so many men triggered the baby boom, which kept many mothers at home tending their children; the postwar migration to the suburbs led to increased conformity and domesticity in American society (the "happy housewife" image).

164. Answers should include reasonable hypotheses that correlate immigration numbers with significant events in both U.S. and world

history—for example, wars, economic depressions, industrial booms or expansions, and so on.

165. Many of the African Americans who migrated north after the war were illiterate laborers. They encountered enormous cultural and economic difficulties in the North, where they were generally segregated and had trouble finding employment. At the same time, many urban whites were migrating out of the cities into suburbia, leaving the cities with large concentrations of poor black residents. Continuing unemployment in African-American communities led to all-black public housing projects, welfare dependency, gangs, drugs, and violence, with no seemingly reasonable remedies offered by the white establishment.

166. South Korea: Osan, Pusan, and Seoul. North Korea: Chipyong, Chongchon River, and Yudam-ni. Soyang is on the border between the two nations.

167. Answers will vary, although it is generally agreed that the United States is globally known as a consumer culture.

168. Answers should include at least some of the following: the baby boom necessitated a surge in the need for consumer products like diapers, playpens, baby carriages, etc., as well as in children's clothing and toys; there was a large increase in the purchase of new (and bigger) cars; there was a greater need for pediatricians and medicines; towns and cities had to build more schools, housing, utilities, etc.; there was an increased demand for teachers and books. As baby boomers aged, there was a significant "bulge" in the number of students trying to gain admission to colleges, leading to increased competition; this difficulty was echoed in the job and affordable housing mar-

ket as students graduated from college and entered the workforce. Finally, the retirement years of the baby boom generation are causing severe stress to the nation's Social Security and Medicare funds, health insurance providers, and elderly care facilities.

169. Most students will probably comment on the still relatively homogeneous quality of American suburbs.

170. During the Great Depression, many people left urban areas and returned home to family farms. This offset immigration numbers for the same period of time. The increase between 1940 and 1950 reflects the return of many American war veterans who went to the cities seeking jobs, as well as an influx of immigrants from war-torn countries in Europe. The percentage passes 50 percent in 1920 as a reflection of the industrial boom in the United States in the late nineteenth and early twentieth centuries.

171. Malcolm X was an African-American activist who espoused political power for black Americans. He shook off a life of crime and joined the Black Muslims, a religion that brought black Americans into closer touch with their African roots and gave them a sense of cultural identity. (The X in his name symbolizes the "lost" African name he never knew.) Malcolm X helped bring about the "black pride" movement; in fact, the now commonly accepted term *African American* came from him. He was assassinated in 1965.

172. Civil Rights Act of 1964—the most comprehensive civil rights legislation in history; outlawed racial discrimination in public places; allowed federal lawsuits for cases of school segregation; outlawed job discrimination based on race, gender, religion, or ethnicity; protected voting rights. Housing and Urban